Surviving the Job Search

Surviving the Job Search

The Ultimate Job-Search Guide: Easy to read, and simple to put into practice

A thirty-year veteran recruiter walks you step-by-step through the résumé, search, and interview process.

Jane Snipes

Surviving the Job Search. © 2020 by Jane Snipes.

All rights reserved.

Printed in the United States of America.

Cover design by Elite Authors.

No portion of this book may be reproduced in any form, except for brief quotations in reviews, without written permission from the author.

For information, send mail to Northstar Recruiting, Inc., PO Box 5916, Florence, SC 29502

ISBN-978-1-7352210-0-7 (Print format)

ISBN-978-1-7352210-9-0 (eBook format)

To God goes all the glory

Table of Contents

Preface ... ix

Writing the Résumé

My Message to You ... 1
An Overview of Basic Job-Search Terminology ... 2
Stuff You Might Have Wondered About ... 4
Overall Page Formatting ... 7
Contact Information ... 10
Basic Setup ... 19
Professional Summary ... 22
Employment ... 28
Education ... 42
Spacing ... 46
Page Naming ... 51
References ... 52
General Tips for Résumés ... 53
Cover Letters ... 56

Conducting the Job Search

Why Are You Searching ... 59
Managing the Roller Coaster of Emotions ... 60
How to Manage Your Nerves ... 62
How to Begin the Search ... 63
Handling the Compensation Question ... 69
Voicemail ... 70
Basic Phone Etiquette ... 71
LinkedIn ... 73

	Where to Find Job Opportunities	77
	How to Work with Third-Party Recruiters	78
	General Résumé Submissions	81

Navigating the Interview

	You Got a Response!	83
	Preparing for the Interview	84
	Attire	90
	Questions You Can Ask	92
	Questions You Might Be Asked	94
	Putting Lipstick on a Pig	100
	The Elephant in the Room	101
	Don't Use the "R" Word	102
	After the Interview	103
	Thank-You Notes	104
	Why You May Not Get the Job	105
	The Non-compete Agreement	108
	The Offer	109
	Resigning	112
	Job-Hopping	113
	You're a Young Adult Just Starting Out	114
	A Note from Jane	115
	Job Search Daily Activity Log	117
	Acknowledgements	119

Preface
I Am Not a Big Fan of Self-Help Books

I've never been a big fan of self-help books. More often than not, an author has outlined ideas beautifully in the first chapter, then spent the next three hundred pages rehashing chapter 1. Unfortunately, I have the attention span of a gnat, so I never finish reading the book. With this in mind, then, my goal here is brevity.

If you've picked up this book, then you (or someone you know) likely need guidance with a résumé or a job search. The process definitely can be daunting, and even perennial optimists can cycle through a roller coaster of emotions a dozen times an hour. One minute you're on the top of the mountain welcoming the chance to change… the next, you're falling into a deep dark pit with no safety net.

This is where I can help. The résumé-writing and job-search processes are the same, regardless of whether you're entry level or executive suite, and after thirty years of recruiting, I know how to steer through the maze and avoid common pitfalls. There are three phases to this process: writing the résumé, conducting the job search, and navigating the interview. I'd like to walk you through each step as quickly and smoothly as possible.

Are you ready? Let's get started.

My Message to You

Life in the Hallway
There's that useless phrase that people love to use: "When one door closes, another door opens." That's so cliché and of zero comfort to you if you're the one staring at a door that's just been slammed in your face. No amount of pounding on that door is going to make it reopen, so you end up stuck in the hallway.

How do you get out of that hallway? You get up, you get dressed, you show up, and you do the work. There are no secret shortcuts, and there is no magic elixir, but through the daily grind, progress *will* materialize. You'll become more practiced at the tasks and will gain emotional muscle memory, which will help you feel more comfortable as you navigate through each phase.

There *is* a new job out there for you, and a new door *will* open. It might be a little uncomfortable in the hallway for a while, but you won't be there forever.

The Endgame
You were born with a set of gifts and talents that are completely unique to you, and through life's journey you're meant to figure out what those gifts and talents are and then use them to help others.

If you don't know what your gifts and talents are, it doesn't mean you don't have any…it just means you haven't discovered them. Yet.

It's Okay to Stumble
It's okay to teeter, stumble, or wobble. Every misstep is a lesson in what *not* to do, and knowing what not to do is way more than 50 percent of the battle. In fact, knowing enough to avoid making a bad decision can be even more valuable than making an accidental good decision.

Tie your self-worth to your potential, not your failure. In fact, just kick failure to the curb altogether and consider that there is no such thing as failure; there is only "next time."

You Don't Need a Lighter Burden; You Just Need a Stronger Back
Tell the world to "Just bring it!"

You are *more* resilient and *more* prepared than you realize, and you *will* triumph. The greater the difficulty, the more compelling your success story, so be brave and be bold. It is going to be amazing!

 Hard work beats talent when talent doesn't work hard.
—Kevin Durant

Stories from the Trenches…

This is from an application in the early 1990s. Companies were permitted to ask gender, so the question was "Sex."

Expected answers were Male or Female, but one applicant wrote, "Yes, once in Philadelphia."

An Overview of Basic Job Search Terminology

Résumé (pronounced "REZ-uh-may")
This is the document used to communicate your skills, education, and experience to prospective employers.

CV
It stands for curriculum vitae and is the same thing as a résumé. In the United States, we use the term résumé. If you're in academia, this document is termed curriculum vitae…or CV for short.

Candidate
This is the person who's being considered for a particular job vacancy. You become a candidate once you have been identified as someone who matches a job and you've indicated interest in being considered for that job.

Hiring Manager
It's the person who decides who gets the job offer. It's typically the direct supervisor, but sometimes the ultimate decision can be made by someone higher up in the organization.

Screener
This is the gatekeeper who reviews résumés and then decides who moves forward in the process. It might be a recruiter, talent acquisition specialist, HR manager, third-party recruiter, the actual hiring manager, the hiring manager's boss, or the hiring manager's assistant. It's basically anyone who looks at a résumé and decides what to do next.

Recruiter
A recruiter can be internal or external to the hiring company. An internal recruiter is employed by the hiring company and typically works in the human resources department. An external recruiter is an independent third party who conducts a search for candidates on behalf of the hiring company.

Headhunter
It's the slang term for a third-party recruiter. Some recruiters get insulted when they're called a headhunter, but the term might have practical origins. During the Great Depression, jobs were scarcer than hens' teeth, so hundreds of people might gather outside a personnel manager's office to vie for a day's work. The personnel manager would scan a sea of faces and point to those he wanted to hire. He hunted for heads in the crowd…he headhunted. I don't know if this is the true origin, but it certainly sounded logical to me.

 If everyone's always in agreement, somebody's lying.

> **Stories from the Trenches…**
>
> A reply on LinkedIn regarding interest in a new opportunity: "Depends on location and salary. I'm pretty happy where I am now but lactating and salary could change my mind."

An Overview of Basic Job-Search Terminology

Applicant Tracking System
It's the database that stores all the candidate information. Every recruiting firm uses one, and it's a safe bet that most hiring companies do too.

When you submit your résumé to a company, the applicant tracking system captures your name, address, email, and phone number and creates a candidate profile on you. When recruiters (in-house or third-party) search that system for candidates, they create a list of pertinent words, then the applicant tracking system generates a list of people whose résumés contain those words.

There are so many versions of these tracking systems and document types (Word, PDF, RTF) that a mistranslation can sometimes occur when a résumé is uploaded into a tracking system. To reduce the chance of any mistranslation happening, we're going to leverage formatting.

Going forward, I'll refer to the applicant tracking system as the *database*.

Key Word
It can be any informative word that describes your role and responsibilities. The person conducting a search for candidates will choose pertinent words from the job description, then search a database for résumés that match those words. These pertinent, or chosen, words are called key words.

 If you're late in your career and are pondering the possibility of getting into a sales role, consider this: If sales was the right place for you, you'd probably have gravitated to it a long time ago.

> **Stories from the Trenches...**
>
> A candidate was considering a role that would have increased her salary by twenty to thirty percent in the first year. I sent her a rather lengthy questionnaire from the hiring manager, and she had this emphatic response when I asked if she'd have time to work on it over the weekend: "On the weekend, I have a life!"

Stuff You Might Have Wondered About

How Does a Recruiter Get Paid?
The recruiter's fee, often called a service fee, is paid by the hiring company.

What Types of Searches Are Used by Third-Party Recruiters?
There are three types: retained, exclusive, and contingent.

In a retained search, the recruiter conducts a search for candidates. The hiring company also forwards to the recruiter all résumés that have been submitted directly to the company. The recruiter screens all candidates and is guaranteed the fee, since it doesn't matter from where the winning candidate originates.

An exclusive search is when a hiring company promises a recruiter that no other third-party recruiters will work on the search, either for an agreed-upon amount of time or for the entire search. This type of agreement gives the recruiter a head start, but it doesn't guarantee the fee, since the ideal candidate might apply directly to the company or might end up being sourced by another recruiter later on.

The contingent search is pretty much a free-for-all, and there could be any number of recruiters working on the same search. The winner of the service fee is the recruiter whose candidate is hired.

How Do You Get in Touch with a Third-Party Recruiter?
Just email your résumé and introduce yourself. More on this later.

Should You Ever Pay the Recruiting Fee?
Nooooooo! Don't listen to any recruiter who says it's your responsibility to pay the fee. If a recruiter says you have to pay, then you should run, not walk, to the nearest exit.

Should You Pay a Recruiter to Conduct Your Job Search for You?
Again, no! The person most qualified to conduct your job search is you. While I absolutely do encourage you to utilize third-party recruiters, your job search shouldn't cost you much more than a ream of paper, some printer ink, and maybe an upgraded LinkedIn membership.

Should You Use a Résumé-Blast Service?
Don't waste your money. Email blast services will email your résumé to a boat load of companies, but those emails will likely be viewed by the recipients as spam, and your résumé will mostly go unopened. You'll be out of pocket on the fee with no job-search progress to show for it, so just keep your money and conduct your own search.

 Good manners come from common sense, and you need both to succeed.

> **Stories from the Trenches...**
>
> An operations manager listed this on his résumé: "Over seed and ran day to day operations."

Stuff You Might Have Wondered About

Do People Still Read Résumés?
Yes…and no. If you define "reading a résumé" as reading every single word, then "no." Screeners will "eyeball" a résumé for key words, then do a deep dive into a sentence or paragraph when something piques their interest. Just by eyeballing through a résumé, though, a screener will be able to generate a mental picture of who you are and what you do. If you're not deemed a match, it can be difficult to be reconsidered, which is why a well-written résumé is so crucial.

What Is the Difference between a Résumé Writer and a Résumé Reader?
A résumé *writer* crafts a résumé from scratch or wordsmiths an existing résumé but isn't the individual actually conducting a search for candidates. A résumé writer knows how to make a résumé look visually appealing but doesn't necessarily understand how a résumé reader or screener will perceive the information or how a database will translate it in the upload process.

A résumé *reader* is someone who looks at résumés with the goal of finding candidates who match given job criteria. I'm a résumé reader and have looked at what must be over a million résumés and LinkedIn profiles over a thirty-year career, so I've become pretty opinionated regarding what works (and what doesn't).

Do You Even Need a Résumé, and What Does It Get You?
There are those lucky few who haven't needed a résumé up to now. Maybe they've worked for a single employer and have risen through the ranks. Maybe they've been able to land new jobs just based on who they knew. These situations, however, are not the norm, and most hiring companies require a résumé in order to gauge skills, experience, and achievements. Since past behavior is a predictor of future performance, people will draw conclusions about your future potential based on what they see in your résumé.

 Be modest in your attire, humble in your communication, and accurate on your résumé.

> **Stories from the Trenches…**
>
> Someone described his company's products as a "God awful offering."

Stuff You Might Have Wondered About

What Is the Difference between a One-Page Summary and a Detailed Résumé?
When I receive a one-page résumé from a mid- to late-career individual, it usually comes with the explanation that the full-on résumé version was too long and that someone along the way had suggested going with a one-page summary instead. The issue with the one-pager, though, is that when you try to cram twenty years of experience onto a single page, it looks claustrophobic, lacks substance, and doesn't let the reader see your true breadth of experience, so you might end up getting kicked out of consideration erroneously.

In order to get the full picture of a candidate, I prefer the more detailed résumé version, and here is a guideline.

Just out of high school: Your résumé will likely be one page.
Just out of college: You'll likely have a one-pager unless you worked during school. Then you might need the second page.
Extensive work experience: You'll be needing that second page to paint the full picture of who you are.

To avoid your being sidelined too soon, we'll aim to create the full résumé version.

Who Is Your Audience?
It's anyone who needs to learn about your professional and educational background.

To cater to the broadest audience possible, I recommend structuring your résumé so it easily can be understood by someone who has little to no knowledge of your industry, company, or function.

Picture this scenario: A temporary employee arrives at a brand-new assignment in the Human Resources department. After being shown the locations of the coffeepot and the restroom, the temp is asked to go through a batch of résumés and identify those which match a particular job description. If the temp has no knowledge of the job, the department, the company, the products, or the industry, this task becomes purely about matching up key words. The temp will review the description, write a few key words on a Post-it note, stick that note to the side of the computer screen, and then start eyeballing résumés. If the required key words are not easily found on a résumé, that résumé will get passed over.

To capture as much attention as possible, we'll aim to have key words that are in plain sight, easy to read, and quickly communicated.

 We tend to adjust our behavior depending on who we're around; with one set of friends, we're one way, and with another group, we act differently. We end up with multiple versions of ourselves, and it is exhausting having to morph from one version to the next. Why not just pick the best version of you, and be that person all the time?

> **Stories from the Trenches…**
>
> One professional spent eight hours interviewing with a company. He even interviewed with the janitor. This was an amazing demonstration of how the company valued *every* employee, no matter their role.

Overall Page Formatting

Should You Use a Template to Write a Résumé?
Templates are actually more trouble than they're worth, so I recommend avoiding them like the plague.

For sure, it is much easier to fill in the blanks and have a lovely, colorful finished product appear at the push of a button, but don't be fooled by the bright and shiny résumé promised you.

There is no guarantee the template résumé will upload properly into a database. The formatting behind the scenes can get corrupted, and information can get dumped into the wrong database field or even omitted completely.

Another issue occurs when you want to add new information to your résumé; the template's behind-the-scenes formatting makes it impossible for you to replicate the spacing, so you'll either give up on the résumé altogether and start over or put up with inconsistent formatting. Neither option is appealing, since both leave you with a less-than-ideal résumé.

The easiest way to create your résumé is to start from scratch in a brand-new Word document. You'll have more control, be less frustrated, and be far better served in the long run.

Tried and True Formatting
After looking through countless résumés, these are my preferences.
- Arial or Calibri font, sized 9 or 10 for the body of the text.
- Slightly larger, bolded, and capitalized font for headings and section titles.
- Regularly spaced font throughout (no expanded or condensed text).
- Single line spacing throughout, with blank lines used to create space between sections.
- Bullets to list information.
- Indents to create an outline format.

How to Get Started
On your personal computer, open up a new Word document and save it.

Do Not Keep Your Résumé on Your Work Computer!
This is your employer's computer, so the company can check it at any time—and it won't look good if your résumé is stored there.

Also, if you get terminated and your laptop is confiscated, you can't retrieve your résumé. So always, always, always keep your résumé on your own machine.

And save your work every few sentences! You do not want to forget this step!

If you already have a résumé and just want to refresh the look, you can get rid of all the formatting by copying and pasting the entire document into a plain text email. This will wash away all formatting and leave you with just the words, which you can then copy and paste into a brand-new Word document. The text is now sanitized and ready to be formatted as desired.

Stories from the Trenches...

An entry-level software developer's goal was to "Liberate mankind from having to labor."

Overall Page Formatting

Don't Use a Table as a Primary Formatting Tool
It might seem as if using a table would make it easier to maintain, but it won't. Here is a nice looking résumé, and it is easy on the reader's eye.

	Robert M. Smith	
123 Alphabet Street New York, NY 12345		555-123-1234 rmsmith@domain.com
Education	BS Degree from ABC University, New York, NY	
	High School Diploma from ABC High School, New York, NY	
Work Experience	January 2000 to January 2013 Operations Manager ABC Lawn & Garden, New York NY • Ran this 20-employee operation • Responsible for all budgeting • Grew the company from $20K to $1M in annual revenue.	

But here is the table that's needed to create the look: It's complicated to set up and will be annoying to maintain long term.

	Robert M. Smith	
123 Alphabet Street New York, NY 12345		555-123-1234 rmsmith@domain.com
Education	BS Degree from ABC University, New York, NY	
	High School Diploma from ABC High School, New York, NY	
Work Experience	January 2000 to January 2013 Operations Manager ABC Lawn & Garden, New York NY • Ran this 20-employee operation • Responsible for all budgeting • Grew the company from $20K to $1M in annual revenue.	

If you think your existing résumé has been done in table format and you want to find the borders…
- **Click Ctrl+ A to highlight the entire document.**
- **On the Navigation Bar at the top of the screen, choose Borders and Shading.**
- **Choose the All Borders option, and the lines should become visible.**

Stories from the Trenches…

A reference's comment about a job seeker's work ethic: "He was always swilling to get the job done."
Another reference described a job seeker's expertise: "It's not his primary skillet."

Overall Page Formatting

Don't Use Columns

I've started to see more résumés that have a two-column format. While this might look like a cool way to format, it's actually just like the table and will be difficult to maintain long term—plus, there likely will be uploading issues.

Here, Bob's two-column résumé looks nice . . .

VP Operations	Robert (Bob) Smith Atlanta, GA email@email.com 555-555-5555
Profile • Detail, detail, detail, detail, detail, detail. • Detail, detail, detail. • Detail, detail, detail, detail, detail. **Skills** • Detail, detail, detail, detail, detail, detail. • Detail, detail, detail. • Detail, detail, detail. **Education** MBA BS Degree	**Employment** **ABC Company,** Atlanta, GA *Manufacturer* **Apr 2014 to Feb 2020** **VP Operations & Supply Chain** • Detail, detail, detail, detail, detail, detail, detail. • Detail, detail, detail. • Detail, detail, detail, detail, detail, detail. • Detail, detail, detail, detail, detail, detail. **DEF Company,** Atlanta, GA. *Manufacturer* **Mar 2003 to Apr 2014** **Business Unit Manager** • Detail, detail, detail. • Detail, detail, detail, detail. • Detail, detail, detail, detail, detail, detail. • Detail, detail, detail, detail, detail, detail.

. . .but this traditional format is actually much easier on the reader's eye, *and* it'll be easier to maintain going forward

Robert (Bob) Smith
Atlanta, GA • email@email.com • 555-555-5555

Profile
- Detail, detail, detail, detail, detail, detail.
- Detail, detail, detail.
- Detail, detail, detail, detail.

Skills
- Detail, detail, detail.
- Detail, detail, detail, detail, detail, detail.
- Detail, detail, detail, detail.

Employment

ABC Company, Atlanta, GA
Manufacturer
Apr 2014 to Feb 2020
VP Operations & Supply Chain
- Detail, detail, detail, detail, detail, detail, detail.
- Detail, detail, detail.
- Detail, detail, detail, detail, detail, detail.
- Detail, detail, detail, detail, detail.

DEF Company, Atlanta, GA.
Manufacturer
Mar 2003 to Apr 2014
Business Unit Manager
- Detail, detail, detail.
- Detail, detail, detail, detail.
- Detail, detail, detail, detail, detail, detail.
- Detail, detail, detail, detail, detail.

 For easy long-term maintenance, start with a blank page and use indents, returns, and tabs to achieve the look you want.

Stories from the Trenches...

A thank-you note from a candidate whose résumé I'd updated: "This is a much less exciting format...feels like you took my pretty nightgown from Victoria's Secret and replaced it with pajamas with feet. Not nearly as sexy but definitely more functional when it's twenty below."

Contact Information

Avoid Borders
Page borders can sometimes make a page look claustrophobic, so I recommend skipping the border altogether. It'll be one less thing you have to think about.

<table>
<tr><td>

Robert (Bob) Smith
Atlanta, GA • email@email.com • 555-555-5555

<u>Profile</u>
- Detail, detail, detail, detail, detail, detail.
- Detail, detail, detail.
- Detail, detail, detail, detail.

<u>Skills</u>
- Detail, detail, detail.
- Detail, detail, detail, detail, detail.
- Detail, detail, detail, detail.

<u>Employment</u>

ABC Company, Atlanta, GA
Manufacturer
Apr 2014 to Feb 2020
VP Operations & Supply Chain
- Detail, detail, detail, detail, detail, detail, detail.
- Detail, detail, detail.
- Detail, detail, detail, detail, detail, detail.
- Detail, detail, detail, detail, detail.

DEF Company, Atlanta, GA.
Manufacturer
Mar 2003 to Apr 2014
Business Unit Manager
- Detail, detail, detail.
- Detail, detail, detail, detail, detail.
- Detail, detail, detail, detail, detail, detail.

</td><td>

Robert (Bob) Smith
Atlanta, GA • email@email.com • 555-555-5555

<u>Profile</u>
- Detail, detail, detail, detail, detail, detail.
- Detail, detail, detail.
- Detail, detail, detail, detail.

<u>Skills</u>
- Detail, detail, detail.
- Detail, detail, detail, detail, detail.
- Detail, detail, detail, detail.

<u>Employment</u>

ABC Company, Atlanta, GA
Manufacturer
Apr 2014 to Feb 2020
VP Operations & Supply Chain
- Detail, detail, detail, detail, detail, detail, detail.
- Detail, detail, detail.
- Detail, detail, detail, detail, detail, detail.
- Detail, detail, detail, detail, detail.

DEF Company, Atlanta, GA.
Manufacturer
Mar 2003 to Apr 2014
Business Unit Manager
- Detail, detail, detail.
- Detail, detail, detail, detail, detail.
- Detail, detail, detail, detail, detail, detail.

</td></tr>
</table>

 Don't aim for perfection because it's a pipedream. Instead, aim for excellence, and be hard-wired to that standard.

Stories from the Trenches...

Note on an application for employment from eons ago: "I refer to the recent death of the Technical Manager at your Company and hereby apply for the replacement of the deceased Manager. Each time I apply for a job, I get a reply that there's no vacancy but in this case I have caught you red-handed and you have no excuse because I even attended the funeral to be sure that he was truly dead and buried before applying. Attached to my letter is a copy of my CV and his death Certificate."

Contact Information

The Best Order

If you're submitting your résumé to a hiring company or recruiter for the very first time, your résumé will be uploaded to a database, and a candidate profile will be created. By using a straightforward format to list your contact information, you'll ensure your information will land correctly in the appropriate database fields.

Your contact information should include your name, address, phone number, and email address, and it's crucial that all this be accurate, consistently aligned, and easy to read.

Here are some formatting options for your contact information.

>   Robert M. Smith
>   123 Alphabet Street
>   New York, NY   12345
>   555-123-1234 • rmsmith@domain.com

This is a very traditional look with the information centered on the page

> Robert M. Smith
> 123 Alphabet Street • New York, NY   12345
> 555-123-1234 • rmsmith@domain.com

Here, all contact details are left justified.

>   Robert M. Smith
> 123 Alphabet Street   555-123-1234
> New York • NY   12345   rmsmith@domain.com

This format splits the address and the contact information

>   Robert M. Smith
>   555-123-1234 • rmsmith@domain.com
> **Home Address**   **School Address**
> 123 Alphabet Street   Student PO Box 123
> New York, NY   12345   University of ABC
>   Anytown, NY 54321

This format is handy for students who have a temporary address while at school.

Using bullets (•) to separate information is a great way to economize on space. You'll find the bullet symbol under the Insert tab on the navigation bar. The database will recognize the bullet as being used as a separator, so it won't pull the bullet into the database and make it part of your information.

 I don't recommend using the vertical slash (|) as a separator, as it can be visually confused with a lowercase *L* if the spacing is too close together.

> **Stories from the Trenches...**
>
> A candidate said, "I thought I was a smart ass...turns out I was a dumb ass. There's a fine line."

Contact Information

What's in a Name?
How you list your name is important.
   If you go by your first name, then it's simple. These names will load correctly into the database.

> **Robert Peter Smith**   **Robert P. Smith**

If you go by a nickname, then you can use apostrophes or parentheses to indicate your everyday name.

> **Robert "Bob" Smith**   **Robert (Bob) Smith**

   If you go by your middle name, then it gets a bit dicey. If the recruiter uploads the résumé of *R. Peter Smith*, then goes to look up *Peter Smith* in the database, the résumé won't show up, because it was saved under *R. Smith*.

> **R. Peter Smith** — This is how it shows up on the resume

| Name | Smith, R. Peter |

This is how it shows in the database

   The recruiter will be able to find the profile in the database by searching for the phone number or email address, or by doubling back to the original emailed document to get the full name, but that's an extra step. To resolve this potential pitfall, you can drop your first initial and just go with your everyday name, but it is totally your preference.

Location of Your Name Is Important
The database assumes that your name will be the first words on your résumé, so if you list something other than your name in that first location, those words will become your name.
   Here, Bob has a description of himself listed at the very top of his résumé.

> **Business Development Visionary**
> **Robert (Bob) Smith**
> 123 Alphabet Street • New York, NY   12345

When Bob's resume is uploaded into the database, his description becomes his name, while his actual name lands in an address field.

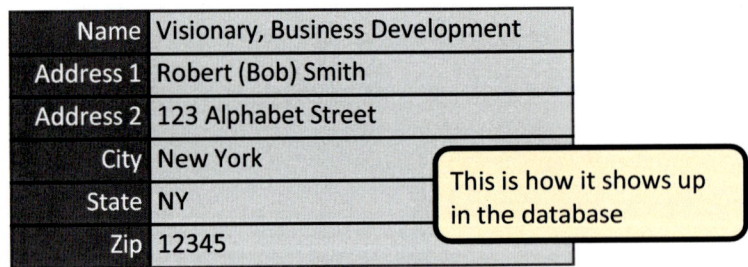

This is how it shows up in the database

 Not knowing what to do isn't a license to do nothing.

Contact Information

Avoid Using Descriptive Words after Your Name

Any credentials or descriptions listed *after* your name can also cause an issue. In this example, Bob is a certified public accountant and lists his CPA credential after his name.

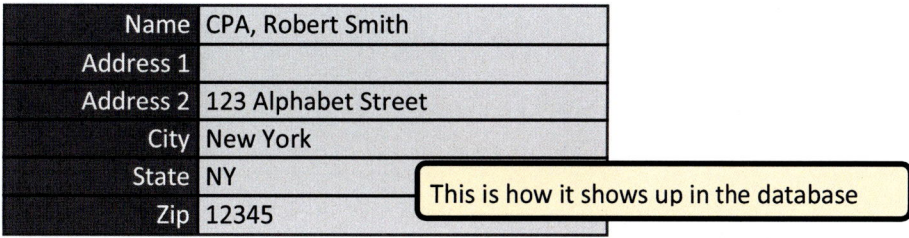

In the upload process, the database made CPA his last name.

Name	CPA, Robert Smith
Address 1	
Address 2	123 Alphabet Street
City	New York
State	NY
Zip	12345

This is how it shows up in the database

To avoid potential issues, just put your credentials on the line underneath your name. Your address might end up being off by a line or two in the database, but at least your name will load correctly.

Your résumé won't get sidelined just because your name didn't load into the database correctly…it just requires an extra step for the recruiter to remedy.

 To ensure you name loads correctly into the database, make sure it's the first thing on the résumé.

> **Stories from the Trenches…**
>
> A midcareer engineer received a great offer from a super company. When I relayed to him the drug screen process he said, "I can't pass that drug test." He smoked pot on weekends, and although he'd skipped a weekend or two so he could pass the screen, this particular company required a hair-follicle test, and there was no way he'd pass it. He had to turn down the offer.

Contact Information

Don't Expand the Text by Using the Space Bar
If you stretch out your name using the space bar, it looks totally fine on the screen and on paper, but the database will recognize the spaces in between the letters and assume the first letter is your *entire* first name, the second letter is your *entire* middle name, and the third letter is your *entire* last name.

In this example, Bob uses spaces to stretch out his name. It looks just fine on the screen and when printed out.

When Bob's résumé is uploaded into a database, however, his name becomes **B, R O**. The database reads **R** *space* **O** *space* **B** *space* and assumes **R** is the first name, **O** is the middle initial, and **B** is the last name. When the database put the name into *LastName, FirstName* format, Bob's name became **B, RO**.

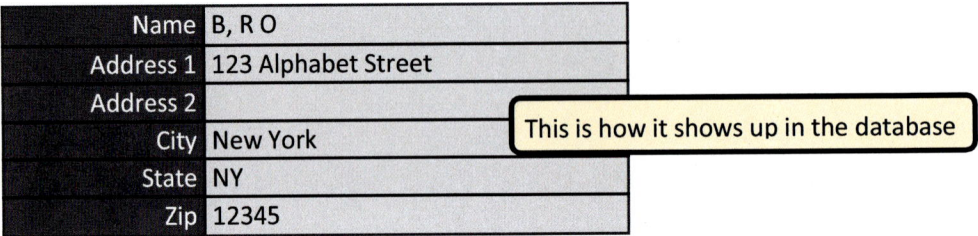

It's also the same for your email address and phone number. The database recognizes the pattern of characters for both and pulls that information, along with your name and address, into your candidate profile in the database. If you expand your email address or phone number using the space bar, that string of characters will no longer match the pattern required, so the information won't register and won't get added to your profile.

Don't Condense Your Text
Condensed font will load correctly into a database because it's a legitimate string of letters. It just might appear a bit weird on the screen or on the printed page, even possibly taking on an entirely different look.

> **Robert R. Smith** becomes RobertRSmith...which isn't too bad.
> A name like **Williams** becomes Wlams...which could be a tad confusing and tough to read.
> **Bill** becomes Bl...and an indeterminate blot on the screen.
> The last name **Burns** becomes Bums...your last name just became *Bums*.

 If you use the "expand font" function in Word, your information will load correctly into the database. Personally, though, I don't like expanded font because I don't think it flows well.

Stories from the Trenches...

An executive said: "I wish he would be succinct in his messaging. There is no need to write a dysentery when you reply to an email."

Contact Information

How Much of Your Address to List

You don't have to list your actual street number and street name, but do list your city, state, and zip code. If you don't specify your geography, a recruiter might ignore your résumé because it'll look like you're not in the desired location. These are options for listing address information.

>   Robert (Bob) Smith
>   123 Alphabet Street
>   New York, NY 12345

This lists the entire address

>   Robert (Bob) Smith
>   New York, NY 12345

This is just City, State, and Zip listed on the same line

>   Robert (Bob) Smith
>   New York
>   NY 12345

This is just City, State, and Zip but on 2 separate lines

What if Relocation Is an Option—or Your Goal?

If you're willing to relocate (or planning to), then it's okay to make a notation on your résumé. Just put it below your contact information so it doesn't get caught up in the database upload process.

>   Robert (Bob) Smith
>   123 Alphabet Street • New York, NY 12345
>   555-123-1234 • bob@domain.com
>   *Relocating to CT February 2020*

>   Robert (Bob) Smith
>   123 Alphabet Street • New York, NY 12345
>   555-123-1234 • bob@domain.com
>   *Willing to Relocate*

>   Robert (Bob) Smith
>   123 Alphabet Street • New York, NY 12345
>   555-123-1234 • bob@domain.com
>   *Open to relocating to the Southeastern US*

 Italicize the relocation notation so it stands out from your contact information.

> **Stories from the Trenches...**
>
> Seen on a resume: "Motivation: wife, 2 young sons, and a mortgage."

Contact Information

Your Email Address Is Crucial

Email is the de facto means of communication these days, so you must list your email address. If you don't, recruiters will just roll their eyes and think, "Really?"

Make sure there aren't any typos in your address, and double-check that you can still access the inbox to retrieve messages.

If you're actively conducting a search, then check that email inbox (plus the spam and junk folders) at least once a day. Don't speak the words "I rarely check that email," because that will make you look sloppy and unorganized.

Always use a professional-sounding address. If you've used *hunkahunkaburninlove* ever since college, then it's time to get a new address. Unless, of course, you're an Elvis impersonator, and then *hunkahunkaburninlove* is entirely appropriate.

A few years ago, I worked with an HR executive who didn't want to view the résumé of anyone who still used an AOL address. She felt it showed a failure to keep up with technology. While I haven't run into that requirement since, it does go to show you just can't predict people's perceptions.

Don't Use Your Work Email for Your Job Search

Never use your work email for your job search because it totally sends the wrong message.

Your current employer might be monitoring your emails and see that you're receiving job inquiries on work time, and there could be fallout from that. I've had candidates (particularly in sales) tell me they were fired because the boss found out they were job hunting.

If you leave your employer, you'll no longer have access to that work email, so you'll miss any incoming messages. Plus prospective hiring managers might see it as a blaring announcement that you see no issue in using company time for personal gain.

Just use your personal email address for your job search; it's a much safer bet.

It's More than Just Your Phone Number...It's Your Lifeline

Always list your phone number too. If you leave it off, you'll just get another eye roll. Make sure the number is correct because one incorrect digit means someone else gets your phone call.

Case in point: There was a highly talented college senior who was sailing through university in three and a half years and was on the road to a super career. He was looking for an internship but, surprisingly, failed to get any responses to his inquiries. Finally, a dedicated HR executive tracked him down. Turns out the young man's phone number was listed incorrectly on his résumé.

 Create a personal email address that's solely dedicated to your job search; that way your regular inbox won't get clogged up with your job-search emails.

Stories from the Trenches...

Spelling errors I've come across: "Goof morning," "My roll was," "I was out sauce."

If your résumé or LinkedIn profile contains the word *pantry*, make sure you don't leave out the *r*. If you've been a *liaison*, don't spell it *lesion*.

Contact Information

Don't Use the Header
It's impossible to predict how a database will react to information in a header: It might read it, or it might not. Here, Bob's contact information is in the header. The title "Education" is below the header.

If the header is ignored, the database will assume the first word on the résumé is the first name. In this case, the only word on that first line is Education, so Education becomes the entire name.

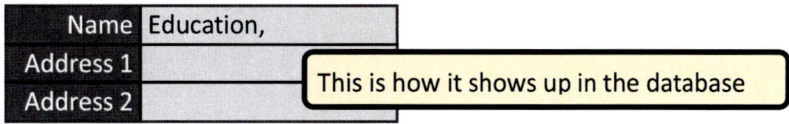

The reverse can also be true. The database might read the header when you don't intend it to be read. Here, the page number is listed in the header, so if the database does read the header, Bob's name becomes *1, Page*.

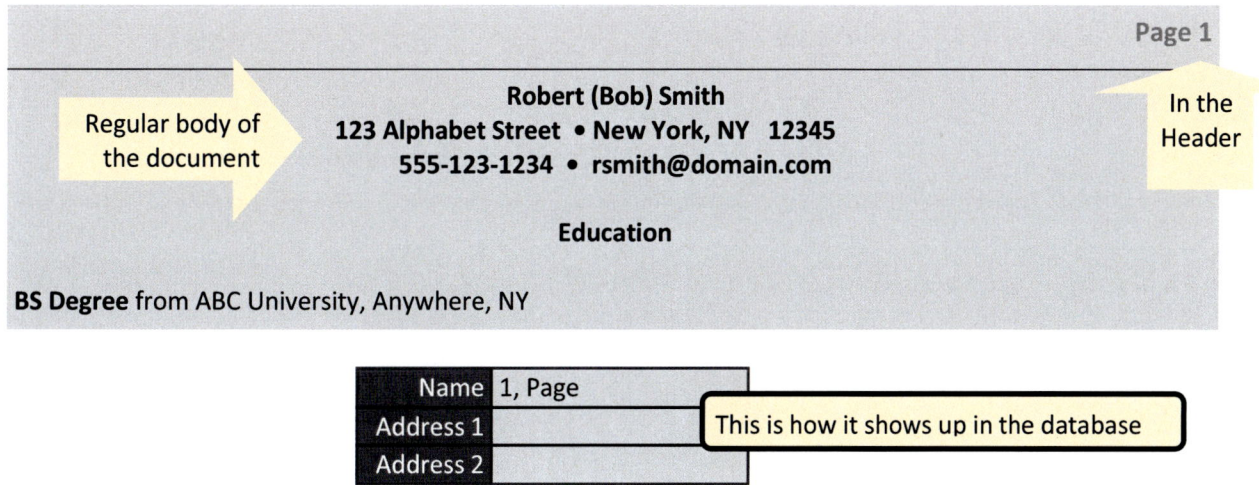

> **Stories from the Trenches...**
>
> Received this reply from a job seeker: "I don't mean to be rude but I have been Americanized. I would not recommend anyone to work for an American Company. I do not know of anyone I would suggest who is desperately in need of a job. I wish you well but would prefer Canada could shove off and paddle to Europe—not sure what the difference is between the USA and Russia."

Contact Information

Text Boxes

Text boxes are like elephants…they're impressive, but they take up soooo much space and are cumbersome to move around.

The issue is they ignore spacing changes and stay in exactly the same place on the page. To move a text box, you physically have to drag it to a new location, and if you're tweaking the spacing a lot, it becomes tedious moving it a millimeter here and a millimeter there.

Here, Education is in a text box.

> **Robert (Bob) Smith**
> 123 Alphabet Street • New York, NY   12345
> 555-123-1234 • rsmith@domain.com
>
> **Education**
>
> **BS Degree** from ABC University, Anywhere, NY

This is a nice setup and it looks good on the page but…

I want to add two extra lines above Bob's name, so I hit Return twice to make the text shift down. Bob's name and address move as desired, but the text box stays in its original location, corrupting the overall look.

> **Robert (Bob) Smith**
> 123 Alphabet Street • New York, NY   12345
> 555-123-1234 **Education** omain.com
>
> **BS Degree** from ABC University, Anywhere, NY

……..when I moved Bob's name and contact information down a few lines, the text moved properly, but the Text Box did not.

This isn't a problem if the spacing is only changed once, but crafting a résumé usually means hundreds of tweaks, so dragging that text box all over creation becomes a tiresome chore. To avoid this, just type your section headings in regular text, and use bold, or a larger font, to make them stand out.

 Avoid using headers and text boxes as much as possible.

> **Stories from the Trenches…**
>
> One candidate said, "Good listening is better than good speaking."

Basic Setup

Résumé Sections

The primary résumé sections are Contact Information, Employment History, and Education.

Additional sections are Professional Summary, Skills, Technology, Academic Research, Patents & Inventions, Publications, Speaking Engagements, and Community Involvement.

There's no set rule that determines the order of the sections. More often than not, the final order is actually driven by the overall spacing needed to make information flow smoothly from one page to the next.

Here's my favorite format. It's clean, concise, easy to follow, and very easy on the eyes. To create this look, I used indents, returns, and bolds to achieve the spacing I wanted.

Name
City, State, Zip · Cell · email address

Education

School Name, City State   **Year**
Degree

Professional Summary

Brief synopsis of industry, skills, and pertinent keywords.

Employment History

Company Name, City, State   **Month Year to Month Year**
A short italicized description of the company (no more than one or two sentences)
Title
- Bullets describing duties, scope of responsibilities, and accomplishments.

Company Name, City, State   **Month Year to Month Year**
A short italicized description of the company (no more than one or two sentences)
Title
- Bullets describing duties, scope of responsibilities, and accomplishments.

Company Name, City, State   **Month Year to Month Year**
A short italicized description of the company (no more than one or two sentences)
Title
- Bullets describing duties, scope of responsibilities, and accomplishments.

> I like to **bold** the **company name, dates, and titles.** If a company description is listed then *italicizing* helps to differentiate it from information about you.

 There are as many ways to format a résumé as there are people writing them, so try a few variations and then go with whatever you like best. If you decide later that you don't like what you have, it's easy to change since there's no behind-the-scenes formatting to wrestle.

Stories from the Trenches…

Received this note from a job seeker: "I have a rabbit of hitting the enter button for spacing."

Basic Setup

Functional versus Chronological

The functional format is trending right now, but it's not easy for a recruiter to gauge the timeline. If someone was a rock star early in their career, those early accomplishments can be made to look as if they're actually more recent, which is deceptive.

This résumé has a functional format, which means all career accomplishments are bunched together, and the Employment section is simply a list of companies.

Robert (Bob) Smith
New York, NY • 555-123-1234 • rsmith@domain.com

Accomplishments

- Over $50M in career sales.
- Won President's Club 5 years.
- Managed a team of 20 and grew sales from $5M to $10M in 2 years.
- Sold enterprise wide/cloud solutions.
- Sold hardware and software security solutions.
- Target markets have been Federal and State Government agencies, and Fortune 1000 companies.
- Led a team of 5 in the start-up environment.

Employment

Jan 2013 to Present	ABC Company, New York, NY.	VP of Sales
Dec 2010 to Dec 2012	CDE Company, New York, NY.	Director of Sales
Aug 2007 to Nov 2010	FGH Company, New York, NY.	Director of Sales

---

Bob's memory will have faded over time. If he's using a functional format, he can't refresh his memory with a quick read of his résumé, because his résumé doesn't contain his accomplishment timeline. It'll be a struggle for him to remember *when* he did *what*, and here's how an initial telephone screen will go.

Me: "When did you manage the team of twenty?"
Bob: "That was at CDE Company."
Me: "When did you win the President's Club awards?"
Bob: "Um...let me think...that was at FGH...no, wait, it was CDE...um...I don't remember...oh wait, yes I do! I won two awards at FGH, one at CDE, and one at ABC...I think. Um...but I could be wrong."

The most practical résumé format is chronological; it's easier and faster to read, a recruiter can see your timeline, and you won't have to struggle to remember details on the fly.
It's a win-win-win!

Stories from the Trenches...

I was coaching a woman who was a resident at a women's abuse shelter. After her interview at a local department store, she sent a thank you note to the store manager saying, "People who say you can't buy happiness obviously don't know where to shop."

She got the job and was the store's #2 sales rep by her third month of employment. Boom!

Basic Setup

Don't Use the Word "I"
Do write your résumé in first-person, but drop the pronouns, particularly "I."

Here's an excerpt from a candidate's résumé. She was a lovely person and not at all self-focused, but using "I" to start every sentence made her appear a bit self-absorbed on paper.

- I have increased sales from…
- I have successfully grown sales…
- I have been awarded…
- I facilitated…
- I have written and presented trainings…
- I have successfully grown retail…
- I have been handpicked…
- I have represented…
- I have proven myself to be…
- I have taken part in 90-day planning sessions…

Instead, write your résumé in first-person, and drop all the pronouns. This achieves three things:
1. It keeps you from appearing narcissistic.
2. It saves space and leaves room for more substantive information.
3. It's faster to read.

A Space Saver
Space is at a premium in a résumé, so here's a nifty trick.

If you want to say, "*I have 5 years' of experience in sales,*" just drop the pronoun and verb, and you're left with "*5 years' experience in sales.*" We saved eight spaces, which doesn't sound like much, but it'll make a big difference cumulatively.

Here are some other examples:

- "I had a team of 10 reporting to me." ➡ "Managed a team of 10."
- "I was tasked with finding additional product enhancements and worked with my customers to determine the requirements they wanted." ➡ "Worked with customers to identify product enhancements."
- "I was responsible for a budget of $2M, and my responsibilities ranged from inventory management to delivery." ➡ "Responsible for a budget of $2M, and managed everything from inventory to delivery."

Should You Include an Objective?
Too narrow an objective might get you tossed out prematurely. Too broad an objective is just a waste of space. Since your overall goal is to land a great job, why use up valuable space stating the obvious? A much better use of this real estate is a summary of key words that provides the reader with a fast and accurate picture of who you are.

 Don't write in third person…it does tend to make one sound rather pompous. Wouldn't one agree?

Stories from the Trenches…

One reference's comment about a candidate's opinions: "I respect him and his onions."

Professional Summary

What to Put in the Summary
The Employment section will contain the finer details of your experience, so just aim for a broad generalization in the Summary section.

Point to the industry you're in: Aviation, transportation, banking, finance, higher education, K–12, retail, government, healthcare, software, manufacturing, retail, landscaping...the list goes on.

Point to your particular discipline: Sales, marketing, product management, product marketing, engineering, operations, customer support, technical support, human resources, administration, teaching, nursing...this list goes on too.

Draw a generalization of your scope of responsibility. For example...
- Hold full operational responsibility and have managed teams of up to 500 across 5 plants.
- Have served as the key holder for major retail operations.
- Teach 5th grade English and responsible for developing entire curriculum.
- Extensive experience working as a cashier in fast-paced retail and restaurant environments.

Point to financial responsibility: For example...
- Have held full P/L responsibility up to $100M.
- Have held budgetary responsibility for marketing.
- Responsible for operational budgets of up to $10M.
- Responsible for reconciling accounts totaling $20K.
- Responsible for setting up the restaurant's cashier stations and reconciling the cash registers.

Point to your core strengths: For example...
- Work with the public and provide professional customer service.
- Expertise in managing cross-functional teams in a highly matrixed global environment.
- Skilled at managing a dynamic classroom environment while fostering an atmosphere conducive to learning.
- An expert in the home and garden retail environment and work with customers to identify trees, shrubs, and flowers that grow best in the planting zone.

What Not to Put in the Summary
Don't list anything that resembles your opinion of yourself, because here's how it'll translate.

Free spirit = undisciplined	**Entrepreneurial** = never finishes anything	**Admired** = a show-off
Visionary = self-absorbed	**Humble** = pretentious	**Persuasive** = bossy
Superior = narcissistic	**High profile** = high maintenance	**World-class** = arrogant
Exceptional = proud	**Multitalented** = scatter brained	**Masterful** = a royal pain
Genius = doesn't value others	**World renowned** = a legend in your own mind	

My all-time favorites are "Serial Entrepreneur," which means you have a really bad case of bright-shiny-object syndrome, and "I'm a prize," which might mean you're really the booby prize.

 It's not always greener on the other side of the fence. Sometimes it's just another shade of brown.

Professional Summary

Be Specific

Aim to paint a clear picture of the accomplishment. Consider these two sentences.

1. Persuasive leader and highly effective communicator with exceptional management skills.
2. Managed a warehouse team of 5; responsible for a budget of $100K; and, in a 12-month period, reduced employee turnover by 90%, decreased costs by 50%, and increased efficiency by 20%.

The first sentence is opinion and just fluff. The second sentence contains facts and carries so much more weight.

 Kindness, like snow, is the great equalizer.

Stories from the Trenches...

A job seeker sent me a résumé with this in the Qualifications/Summary section: "Performance-driven professional seeking a (Position) with (Company / Industry). Strong communication skills combined with the proven ability to build robust relationships and effectively manage competing demands."

Note-to-self...don't customize this section with fill-in-the-blanks. It's a recipe for disaster.

Professional Summary

How to Craft the Summary
The easiest way to write the summary is to just start typing. This is the rough draft phase, so do a brain dump and just throw stuff on the page as it comes to mind. You'll refine and polish into a concise write-up as you go. The aim is to give a brief overview of your skills, so list key words that accurately represent your industry and scope of responsibility—and how your employers have benefited from having you on the team.

Avoid describing yourself in flowery terms (masterful, visionary, noteworthy, world-class) because it's not what you think of yourself that's important—it's the results you've gained for your company or your clients that make you valuable to a prospective employer.

Don't take up space mentioning your communication skills or organizational abilities, as those skills will be implied through the accomplishments you list. Above all, be sensible, be humble, and be accurate.

Narrative or Bullets
I vote for bullets, because it's so much easier to glance through and pick up pertinent key words. Compare these two examples.

Summary

> Example 1
> This is a long run-on sentence with items separated by semi-colons.

Seasoned sales representative in the healthcare sector; primary focus on small and medium regional hospitals; call on Facilities Managers and C-Level executives; sell physical and logical security solutions; products include Access Control, CCTV, IP Video, Surveillance, Readers, Biometrics, and ID Management; carry a quota of $2M and have exceeded quota 8 out of the last 10 years; awarded President's Club 7 consecutive years from 2006 to 2012.

Summary

> Example 2
> This is the same information but in bulleted format.

- Seasoned sales representative in the healthcare sector.
- Primary focus on small and medium regional hospitals.
- Call on Facilities Managers and C-Level executives.
- Sell physical and logical security solutions.
- Products include Access Control, CCTV, IP Video, Surveillance, Readers, Biometrics, and ID Management.
- Carry a quota of $2M and have exceeded quota 8 out of the last 10 years.
- Awarded President's Club 7 consecutive years from 2006 to 2012.

The wording is exactly the same in both, but the bulleted example is easier and faster to read.

 A degree may not be required, but honesty and integrity are.

> **Stories from the Trenches...**
>
> Got this note back on LinkedIn: "1:00pm works best for me. I also immediately called you back once I kissed your phone call. I was in the middle of getting my toes replaced on my car."

Professional Summary

Some Formatting Examples

You have a ton of options and can mix and match the formatting depending on the information you want to relay. Here are some examples.

Qualifications Profile

> **Example 1**
> You can call this section something other than Summary if you want to.

Strong product and application knowledge of Aeronautical navigation systems. Serve as the technical expert in the sales process and have supported up to 10 sales reps. Generate quotations and technical proposals, respond to RFPs and RFIs, conduct technical sales presentations, and assist the implementation team with deployment and customer sign-off.

Summary

> **Example 2**
> This section doesn't have to be lengthy.

A driven sales professional motivated by sales results and by building connections with customers. Experience with cold-calling and calling on residential customers to identify new business opportunities.

Executive Profile

R&D Management / Operations / Strategic Planning / Product Management / Technology Architecture
Turnaround Management / Relationship Management

- 20+ years experience leading Hardware and Software Development teams to deliver products and solutions in the Consumer Electronics market; extensive expertise in technology development, operations, management, strategic business planning, and partner/supplier negotiations.
- Expertise in micro electronics servicing markets requiring highly reliable, rugged, and small footprint electronic solutions.
- Leverage global engineering resources including contract manufacturing and complex international multi-site R&D projects.
- Lead teams from concept through product launch and maturity; minimizing time to market, cost, and complexity while maximizing performance and marketability.
- Participate in the sales process articulating complex technology and business value to customers and investors.
- Experience in both corporate organizations and venture funded start-ups.
- Proven record of generating year-over-year revenue increases of over 20%.

> **Example 3**
> You can get creative and combine a keyword section plus have bullets for added detail

 Keep the summary short enough so that the description of your current role fits entirely on the first page. You want to avoid having a page break in the middle of a list of bullets.

Stories from the Trenches...

A hiring VP summarized her philosophy: "You can be on the bus or under it. Just pick your position"

Professional Summary

Here are some more formatting examples.

> **Example 4**
> Categorizing information is helpful

EXECUTIVE LEADERSHIP	OPERATIONS MANAGEMENT	SUPPLY CHAIN/LOGISTICS
Strategic Planning & Integration	Prospect Research & Analysis	Inventory Control Processes
Change Management	Industrial Engineering	Logistics Integration
Vision & Leadership Expertise	Budget & Database Management	Distribution Management
Team Building & Training	Risk & Opportunity Tracking	Continuous Process Improvement
In-Depth Business Acumen	Project Lifecycle Oversight	Production Oversight
Financial Analysis	Lean Manufacturing	Purchasing Negotiations

> **Example 5**
> Short and sweet works well

Senior Operations Manager

Innovative team builder and problem solver with over twenty years of manufacturing and logistics management experience leveraging a strong technical background to lead innovation and improvement.

OPERATIONS • PRODUCTION • LOGISTICS • SUPPLY CHAIN MANAGEMENT

Management professional with experience in operations and production management. 15+ years running the operations of manufacturing and warehouse facilities. BS in Business Management. Demonstrated track record of outstanding performance and delivering results by excellent planning, cost savings, and process and productivity improvements.

- Production Planning
- Materials Planning
- Vendor Management
- Project Management
- Logistics Planning
- Customer Care Relations
- Budgeting
- PowerPoint, Excel, Word, AS/400
- Team Building
- Process Improvement
- Human Resource Support

> **Example 6**
> Combining a short narrative with columns can be highly effective

Summary of Qualifications

- Results Oriented Sales and Business Development Leader with over 10 years of documented success.
- Adept at planning and executing programs to cultivate opportunities for business and revenue growth.
- Conducting detailed analyses of current and future industry trends, competitive product and service offerings, and gathering market intelligence and developing assessments.
- Project-managing all phases of business development initiatives while identifying new client prospects.
- Establishing strong business relationships and securing audiences with decision-makers.
- Conducting effective sales presentations, and closing both new accounts while retaining existing clients.

> **Example 7**
> Just load up on keywords for the best overall affect

 The Summary is a high overview, but you'll likely end up including some specific achievements, so make sure to list those same achievements in the appropriate Employment section. This will ensure each employment entry provides a complete picture of your skills and expertise.

Professional Summary

Here Is Where a Table Is Very Useful
If you have a list of bullets, a table can be a marvelous way to save space. An added bonus is that tables respond to spacing changes, so editing won't be as tedious as it is with text boxes.

- Marketing & Sales
- Project Management
- Sales Force Management
- Channel & Reseller Sales
- Briefing/Proposal Generation
- Federal and Direct Sales
- Large Scale Contract Negotiation
- Over $50M in career sales-to-date
- Annual quota of $3M
- Enterprise wide/cloud solutions
- ID Management, Smart Card, and Security Applications
- Law Enforcement & Criminal Justice Applications

In this example, 12 bullets require 12 lines.

• Marketing & Sales	• Large Scale Contract Negotiation
• Project Management	• Over $50M in career sales-to-date
• Sales Force Management	• Annual quota of $3M
• Channel & Reseller Sales	• Enterprise wide/cloud solutions
• Briefing/Proposal Generation	• ID Management, Smart Card, and Security Applications
• Federal and Direct Sales	• Law Enforcement & Criminal Justice Applications

If we use a two-column table, we only need six lines to list the same 12 bullets.

• Marketing & Sales	• Federal and Direct Sales	• ID Management, Smart Card, and Security Applications
• Project Management	• Large Scale Contract Negotiation	• Law Enforcement & Criminal Justice Applications
• Sales Force Management	• Over $50M in career sales	
• Channel & Reseller Sales	• Annual quota of $3M	
• Briefing/Proposal Generation	• Enterprise wide/cloud solutions	

If we use a three-column table, we only need five lines to list the same 12 bullets.

Don't Use Invisible Key Words
A few years ago, it became popular to throw a key word dump in white font onto the bottom of a résumé. The words were invisible to the reader but would be recognized by the database when uploaded. It was supposed to ensure the résumé would be selected more often, and it was a fairly decent idea in theory, but if the font color happened to change to something other than white, the word dump became visible on the page and looked bizarrely out of place. If a key word is worth including, go ahead and list it in your summary.

Keep the table lines visible while you perfect the formatting. After you're satisfied, make the lines invisible for a cleaner, neater look.

> **Stories from the Trenches…**
>
> Received this reference on a candidate: "She's honest, ethical, and always processional in her approach."

Employment

It's tough to remember what you've done and even tougher to write about it, which is why this section makes people procrastinate and put off writing a résumé until, like, next year.

If we break down the task into components and put some structure in place first, though, it's so much easier to fill in the details.

Basic Information Needed
- Company name
- Employment dates—months *and* years (more on this later)
- Job title and responsibilities

Optional Information
- The city and state in which your office was located, or the state in which you lived during your tenure
- A one-line description of the company
- Your reason for leaving the role

Font Size
My favorite font for résumés is Arial or Calibri, because they're easy on my old eyes. My favorite font size is 9 or 10, but this can increase depending on how the overall spacing ends up. For now, though, we won't worry about overall font size. Just type away and get the information on the page.

Format
This is my favorite employment format because it's easy to follow the path from one job to the next.

> **Company Name,** City, State   **Month Year to Month Year**
> *Short description of the company (no more than one or two sentences)*
> **Title**
> - Bullets describing duties, scope of responsibility, and accomplishments
> - More information
> - More information

I used indents, bolding, and italics to create this look.

> The magic of writing isn't so much in the writing…it's in the editing. Don't stress over the exact wording now. Just get your thoughts on paper, and you can refine and polish later. If you want to gauge how your words come across, read them out loud.

> **Stories from the Trenches…**
>
> Asked a candidate, "What's your ideal job?" He said, "Find a Sugar Momma."

Employment

What if You Don't Like the Suggested Format?
That is totally okay! You have a ton of options and can format any way you like. Just make sure all employment entries are in the exact same format so it looks uniform. Here are sample formats you can try.

Month Year to Month Year	**Company,** State, City	**Title**
Company, State, City	**Title**	**Month Year to Month Year**
Month Year to Month Year	**Title**	**Company,** State, City
Title	**Company,** State, City	**Month Year to Month Year**

How to Accommodate Multiple Roles within the Same Company
Just put the company name and your complete work date on one line, then list each role underneath. Adding in dates for each individual role is optional.

> **ABC Company,** New York, NY   **January 1990 to May 2010**
> **Director,** December 2000 to May 2010
> - Bullets describing duties, scope of responsibility, and accomplishments.
> - Yada yada yada.
>
> **Manager,** August 1996 to December 2000
> - Blah blah blah.
> - Yada yada yada.
>
> **Supervisor,** June 1992 to August 1996
> - Blah blah blah.
> - Yada yada yada.
>
> **Clerk,** January 1990 to May 1992
> - Blah blah blah.

To emphasize multiple roles within a single company, underline the company name and the overall dates of employment, then list underneath all the roles you held within that company

> *It's easy to take your own skills for granted and to forget the difference your work makes in the lives of your colleagues, customers, and vendors, so think broadly about your work. The skills you value least about yourself might be those that are valued most by others.*

Stories from the Trenches...

Seen on LinkedIn: "A sales professional who likes to look good, drink whiskey, and smoke cigars."

Employment

What if Your Company Has Changed Names like Some People Change Underwear?
Your employer might have changed names or ownership, so a notation next to your title is a quick way to show how a company evolved from one entity to the next.

Galactic Behemoth, New York, NY — **Jan 1990 to May 2010**
Director, Galactic Behemoth, December 2000 to May 2010
- Bullets describing duties, scope of responsibility, and accomplishments.
- Yada yada yada.

Manager, National Conglomerate, Inc., (acquired by Galactic Behemoth), August 1996 to December 2000
- Blah blah blah.
- Yada yada yada.

Supervisor, Slightly Larger Corp. (acquired by National Conglomerate, Inc.), June 1992 to August 1996
- Blah blah blah.
- Yada yada yada.

Clerk, Iddy Biddy Company (acquired by Slightly Larger Corp.), January 1990 to May 1992
- Blah blah blah.
- Yada yada yada.

Date Format

There are three ways to represent the month; spell out the name of the month fully, use an abbreviation, or use a numerical format (MM/YY or MM/YYYY). I've used all three formats throughout this book, but my favorite, however, is the three-letter abbreviation.

Jan   Feb   Mar   Apr   May   Jun   Jul   Aug   Sep   Oct   Nov   Dec

I deliberately don't use a period at the end of each abbreviation, because it's too easy for inconsistency to creep in.

This format is crisp, economizes on space, and is quick and easy to read.

January 2nd, 2015	becomes	**Jan 2015**
August 30th, 2002	becomes	**Aug 2002**
October 4th, 2014	becomes	**Oct 2014**

Use any date format that appeals to you—just make sure you're consistent throughout.

Stories from the Trenches...

A candidate with manufacturing experience wanted to indicate he had experience with LEAN, a manufacturing methodology. Unfortunately, he listed he had "Experience with LENA."

Employment

Do You Really Need to List the Months of Employment?
I feel they're needed, and to counter the thousands of others who'll disagree with me, let me present my case.

Prior to the dot.com bubble in 2000 and 2001, employees tended to stay with companies for long periods of time. A gap of a few months in between jobs didn't matter so much because there were typically mega-years of employment on either side of the gap.

In the 1990s, the dot.com era arrived, and with it came the online job boards. Demand for technical expertise went through the roof, and companies were desperate for talent. It was a job-search free-for-all and such a circus that someone could quit their job on a Monday, slap a résumé on the job boards on Tuesday, and be gainfully employed with a healthy raise, a very nice sign-on bonus, and stock options by Friday.

Then the bubble burst. The economy tanked, and companies went belly-up faster than you could say, "May I have a severance, please?" The unemployment rate was staggering, and it became common for people to be unemployed for well over a year. To make their employment look like it had been continuous, people started listing *only* the years they'd been in each role. Check out this example.

If we read these dates from bottom to top, it looks like this person's had continuous employment,

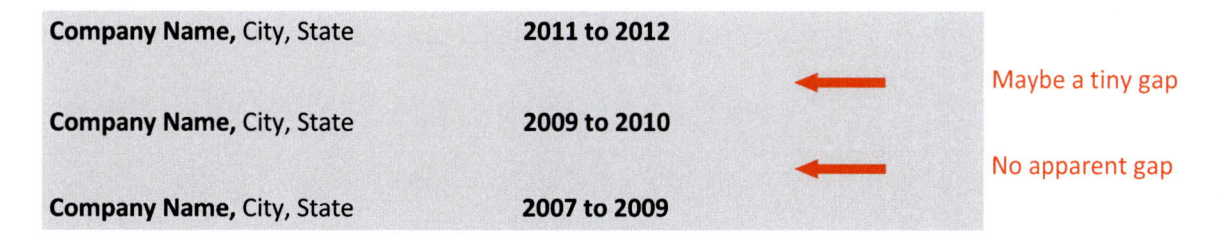

Company Name, City, State	**2011 to 2012**	
		← Maybe a tiny gap
Company Name, City, State	**2009 to 2010**	
		← No apparent gap
Company Name, City, State	**2007 to 2009**	

but if we add in the months, we get an entirely different story.

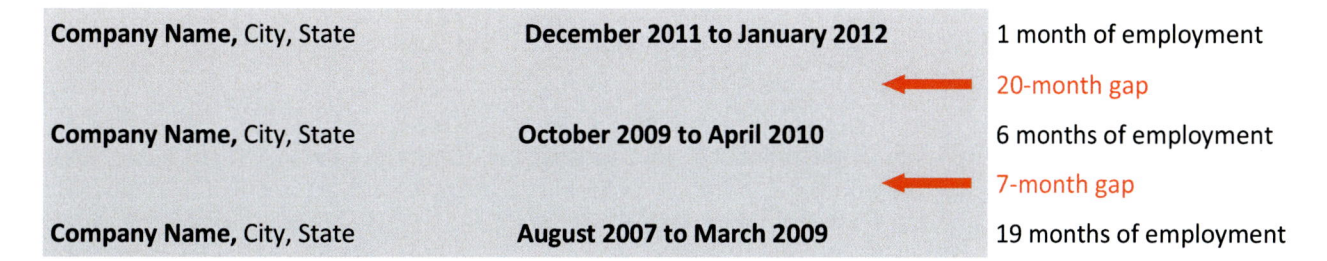

Company Name, City, State	**December 2011 to January 2012**	1 month of employment
		← 20-month gap
Company Name, City, State	**October 2009 to April 2010**	6 months of employment
		← 7-month gap
Company Name, City, State	**August 2007 to March 2009**	19 months of employment

But Does It Really Matter?
As a recruiter, I want to see the months and years of employment. It's not that I don't like gaps; I just want to know where they are and the reasons for them. If you do list them, a reader will see you're being forthright about your history and have nothing to hide. Honesty and integrity win points.

💡 **It's easier to explain a gap than it is to explain an omission.**

> **Stories from the Trenches...**
>
> During the salary negotiation discussion with a hiring manager, a candidate said, "As your sales rep I'll be negotiating for you every day. As a candidate vying for this sales role, today, I'm negotiating for myself. Would you really want to hire a sales rep who doesn't know how to negotiate?"

Employment

How Far Back Do You Go?
Include up to the last twenty years of experience. Résumé writers might rail against this recommendation, but it's impossible for a recruiter to gain a full understanding of your career without seeing your full history.

Here's an example. The CEO of a retail conglomerate has twenty years of experience. Right out of high school, he got a job as the night janitor at one of the stores and took college courses during the day. He worked his way through the ranks at the store, then moved over to corporate. Simultaneously, he earned his associate's, bachelor's, and MBA degrees, all while working full time. If our CEO only lists the last ten years on his résumé, he's just another run-of-the-mill executive. If he goes back to the beginning and shows the path he took from janitor to CEO, it's so much more compelling a story and completely differentiates him from the crowd.

Go ahead and add in those early years, and be proud of them. They're what molded you into who you are today, and they lend credibility to where you are now.

What if You Don't Remember Your Work Dates?
If you're not sure of your work dates, then you have options.
- Call the company's HR or payroll department and ask.
- Check old tax returns.
- Give it your best estimate...but do err on the side of caution. I'd rather see someone underestimate than overestimate an employment duration.

In What Order Do You List Your Employment?
Your most recent employment should be at the top, and your earliest job should be at the bottom. All jobs will then be in descending order based on date.

Company Name	Dec 2010 to Jan 2011
Company Name	Oct 2009 to Nov 2010
Company Name	Aug 2007 to Aug 2009 ✓

Company Name	Aug 2007 to Aug 2009
Company Name	Oct 2009 to Nov 2010
Company Name	Dec 2010 to Jan 2011 ✗

If you deviate from the most-recent-at-the-top format, it'll be confusing for the reader, because their eyes will go straight to the job at the top of the list and assume it's the most current role. Because the dates will be from years prior, there will be a snap conclusion that you've been unemployed since you left. The reader will quickly realize you've flipped the format, but the most-recent-at-the-bottom format goes against the grain and is annoying to read.

💡 *Be accurate in every instance. That way you never have to backpedal or cover your tracks.*

> **Stories from the Trenches...**
>
> One candidate pushed back hard when I wanted to know the months of employment in addition to the years. At one point he said, "I don't remember the month...that was like two years ago already!"

Employment

Do the Dates Match?
Once you've written all the dates down, follow them from the earliest to the most recent to make sure they all match up. If there are overlaps or gaps, can they be explained? Will a reader be able to trace the path you've taken by following the dates from start to finish?

Is It Okay for You to Fudge Dates?
For me, this is an unequivocal no! Fudging dates is lying, and if you can justify doing that to make yourself look good, then what else can you justify? It's far better to list your employment months and years accurately and just let the chips fall where they may.

Is It Okay for a Résumé Writer to Omit Work Experience or Fudge Dates?
This is absolutely not okay either! You own your résumé, and it's your responsibility to ensure everything listed is accurate. If a résumé writer recommends leaving off a particular employment because it'll look better, then you should do an Elvis, and leave the building.

Case in point: An executive-level candidate sailed through the interview process, but in the eleventh hour, the VP of HR noticed date discrepancies between his résumé and application. It turned out that a résumé writer had deleted a fifteen-month employment stint, then fudged the prior and follow-on employment dates to close the gap. The résumé writer was flawed in omitting the information, but it was the candidate's responsibility to make sure his résumé was accurate.

If you are inaccurate in any way, your integrity and judgment will be in question, and that's a bad place to be. If you have short stints, just be honest about them, then be ready to talk about your reasons for leaving each.

What if You Have Overlapping Dates?
It's totally okay. Here we have a two-month overlap between Company B and Company C.

Company A	Dec 2010 to Jan 2011
Company B	Oct 2009 to Nov 2010
Company C	Aug 2007 to Dec 2009

Just accurately list the dates, and be ready to explain the reason for the overlap.

Who's to Know if Your Dates Aren't Entirely Accurate?
Well, no one really…just you and maybe some persnickety recruiter who does a deep dive into work history. Oh, and the HR manager once the background check information shows up.

Case in point: One individual left off an eleven-month consulting stint and changed the end date of the earlier role to make it all blend. He said he'd done it because he didn't want to look like a job-hopper. So instead of looking like a job-hopper, he became a fraud instead. Not a good trade-off.

What Jobs Do You List?
All of them, please, because it reflects your honesty and integrity, and if you have job-hopped, then seeing it on paper might motivate you to settle in and stop moving around quite so much.

> **Stories from the Trenches…**
>
> A comment from a reference regarding a candidate's attention to detail: "It's a disease. My first impression of him was that he was a mad scientist."

Employment

What if You Do Have Major Employment Gaps?
It's not so much the gap that's important; it's your delivery of the explanation of that gap that will be key. If you try to disguise the gap or overly justify it with a lengthy explanation, you'll come across as cagey. If you're candid and provide a quick, simple explanation, it'll put you in a much better light.

Oh, and this is a two-way street, so someone's reaction to your unemployment gap can give you valuable insight into the company culture and how people are viewed. If the recruiter or hiring manager is judgmental and criticizes your reasoning, it could be a reflection of a somewhat toxic work environment.

So don't hide a gap…just reflect it accurately, and keep moving forward.

Reasons for Leaving Each Job
Over your entire career, your reasons for leaving are a direct reflection of your character, your values, and your judgment. For sure, everyone has a mulligan or two (those total disaster jobs that should never have been accepted in the first place), but a lot can be learned about you and how you think based on the total sum of your reasons for leaving.

You do *not* have to list your reasons for leaving, but if you have some quirky twists and turns along the way, listing the reasons for them on your résumé gives you a chance to come up with succinct reasons ahead of time; that way you won't have to think on the fly in an interview.

Company Name, City, State   **Jan 2019 to Present**
Title
- Bullets describing duties, scope of responsibilities, and accomplishments.
- More info

Reason for leaving: The division is closing and future job stability is uncertain.

Company Name, City, State   **Aug 2013 to Dec 2018**
Title
- Bullets describing duties, scope of responsibilities, and accomplishments.
- More info

Reason for leaving: Role was cut in a major downsizing.

Company Name, City, State   **Jan 2013 to Aug 2013**
Title
- Bullets describing duties, scope of responsibilities, and accomplishments.
- More info

Reason for leaving: This was a stop-gap job while conducting a search for a more career-oriented role.

So that you don't take up a lot of space, keep each reason for leaving limited to a single line.
Be consistent throughout. If you list a reason for leaving for one job, then do the same for all jobs.

> 💡 **Use $ and a capital M to denote millions of dollars. For example, ten million dollars is $10M. Don't use 10mm, since that means 10 millimeters.**

> **Stories from the Trenches…**
>
> A candidate's reply when asked about his strengths: "Well, I'm fifty years old and have made it this far."

Employment

The Magic Is in the Wordsmithing
Some situations are incredibly difficult, but if you take the emotion out of the equation, it becomes easier and less risky to say why you left a job.

The truth		A non-emotional perspective
I'd been with my company for 25 years then some new young gun was hired and he started bringing in cronies from his last company. They kicked me and the rest of my team to the curb.	→	Role was cut when a newly appointed executive brought in his own team.
The Engineering team wouldn't listen to what our customers wanted. We were light years behind the competition and I couldn't *give* our product away so I bailed and went to a competitor.	→	The company hadn't invested in new technology and sales were suffering, so I left for a more stable opportunity.
The boss was truly a control freak and people were leaving in droves. I couldn't stay there one more minute!	→	The corporate environment became less team-oriented so I left for a more stable role.
My division was bought and sold 3 times and we were being sold for 4th time. I just couldn't stomach one more go-around so I left.	→	Division was being acquired for the 4th time so left for a more stable opportunity.
I was still in college and the boss quit letting me work around my class schedule so I left.	→	Work schedule overlapped with classes so resigned to focus on school.

The words I want you to take out of your vocabulary right now are *fired* and *terminated*. There's too much negative connotation attached to both, so just erase them from your brain and never speak them again.

If you were fired from your job because you did something wrong, then you were *released* or *exited*. If your job was cut because of cost reductions or restructuring, then you were *downsized*.

> Some employment situations are so painful that it just seems impossible to come up with a neutral reason for leaving, so try writing out what you want to say, then refine the wording until there's no emotion left. To hear how it sounds, speak it out loud and record it. Practice until you can say it with zero bitterness. Above all, keep all your reasons honest, brief, and neutral.

Stories from the Trenches…

A college grad went to a career fair and was told by a major consulting firm's representative never to use the round bullet points on a résumé because only the square ones made it look like you know what you're talking about. Are you kidding me? That has got to be one of the stupidest things I've ever heard. Everyone knows it's only the round bullets that make you look smart. Just kidding!

Employment

Building Out the Employment Details

The best way to start filling in the detail of each Employment section is to do a brain dump and type everything you can think of for each job. Don't overthink this right now—just type anything and everything you can remember. Here are some ideas…

Duties	Projects won	Budgets managed	Quotas
Responsibilities	Projects worked on	Patents awarded	Sales Attained
Scope of work	Accomplishments	Presentations	Accounts retained
Territory	Awards	Tools utilized	New accounts won
Industry verticals	People/teams managed	Instruments utilized	Accounts expanded
Sample customers	Management scope	Software programs	Extra responsibilities earned
Statistics	Expenses reduced	Revenue generated	Timelines met
Deliverables met	Errors corrected	Crises averted	Publications

Creating an Outline

For a crisp, clean result, I've found the outline format is the most efficient way to convey the full story in as few words as possible. Here are some tips for creating an outline.

- Don't use pronouns…*I, my, we, they, our.* Write in first-person with the personal pronouns omitted.
- Limit the use of filler phrases; *such as, and others, in addition to, as an example.* If something is noteworthy, it should be listed, not implied.
- Start sentences with an action verb.

Responsible for	Partnered with	Sold to	Managed
Analyzed	Served	Generated	Called on
Evaluated	Reconciled	Led	Created
Tasked with	Engineered	Manufactured	Supervised

Filling in the Detail

If you're having difficulty coming up with things to write, look over your job description and use it as a framework. For additional ideas, check out your colleagues' LinkedIn profiles and see what they've written. Don't copy verbatim—just use their profiles as a springboard.

Keep in mind, each employment description is a work in progress, so don't beat yourself up if you can't remember everything immediately. Over time, more will come to mind, and you'll edit and polish the outline until you get a clean, crisp overview that highlights what you bring to the table.

> **Going forward, keep a note of your accomplishments on your personal computer. If you're released, rightsized, downsized, or seasonally corrected, and your work computer is confiscated, you'll still have a record of your achievements.**

Stories from the Trenches…

One executive commented: "Insanity is having the same people follow the same process, with the leader expecting different results."

Employment

What Information Should You List?

If you're in sales, talk about...
- Territory
- Customer base and particular accounts gained
- Industry or market vertical focus
- Quotas and actual sales generated
- Troubled accounts you turned around and retained

If you're in operations, talk about...
- Costs you reduced
- Productivity increases achieved
- Improvements in inventory turns and quality
- Reductions in space required
- Decreased time from raw materials through manufacturing to shipping

If you're in product development, talk about...
- Gathering requirements from customers, then translating those requirements for the engineering team
- Identifying new market trends
- Staying ahead of customer requirements
- Shortening the go-to-market time
- Generating additional revenue for the company

If you're in engineering, talk about...
- The industry and related technology
- Products you've helped bring through the R&D process
- Products you've helped bring through the product development life cycle
- Side projects with which you've worked
- Patents awarded

If you're in executive leadership, talk about...
- The size of the team and budget for which you've been responsible
- Functions you've led (operations, sales, production, customer service, technical support, engineering, manufacturing, supply chain)
- Costs reduced and improvements made
- Market gains achieved

You need to tell your full story as accurately as possible but in as few words as possible. Throw all your thoughts on the page, then whittle it down to all primary and secondary responsibilities, activities, and accomplishments—plus any other noteworthy achievements you want to mention.

To Present

If you've already left a company, don't list "to present" as your work date. Inaccurate dates will just make you look sloppy, lazy, or fraudulent...or a combination of all three.

    Case in point: A candidate once listed "to present" in his most recent job but admitted he'd left the role twenty-two months prior. When I pressed him about it, he said a résumé counselor had told him to list "to present."

    Really? That was terrible advice.

*Interviewing is both art and science; **what** you say is the science, **how** you say it is the art.*

Employment

What if You Didn't Always Hit Your Sales Quota?
If you didn't always meet your sales quota, here's a way to show your performance.

Sales Representative
- Territory was the Southeastern US and called on commercial End User companies.
- Clients included Bank of America, Southern Freight, Belk, Carolina Hospital Systems, and Properties R Us.
- Accomplishments:
  * **2012:** Quota of $500K, generated $450K in sales, and achieved 90% of plan.
  * **2013:** Quota of $750K, generated $800K in sales, and achieved 106% of plan.
  * **2014:** Quota of $900K, generated $850K in sales, and achieved 94% of plan.
  * **2015:** Quota of $1M, generated $1.5M in sales, and achieved 150% of plan.

> In this example, a sales rep exceeded his quota in 2013 and 2015.

This sales rep was pretty close to hitting quota in 2012 and 2014, so I recommended listing the quota amounts to show how he'd persevered through to success.

If you don't want to show you missed your quota, then just list the sales you did achieve.

Sales Representative
- Territory was the Southeastern US and called on commercial End User companies.
- Clients included Bank of America, Southern Freight, Belk, Carolina Hospital Systems, and Properties R Us.
- Accomplishments:
  - **2012:** Generated $450K in sales.
  - **2013:** Generated $800K in sales.
  - **2014:** Generated $850K in sales.
  - **2015:** Generated $1.5M in sales.

The goal is to show a consistent pattern of effort and success without being disingenuous in any way.

Listing Percentages Doesn't Always Paint the Full Picture
Listing percentages to detail achievements is great, but it's much more compelling if you also list the number from which those percentages were derived, along with the corresponding time frame.

Compare these two achievements:
- Grew sales 10%.
- Grew sales 10% from $5M to $5.5M over a 6-month period.

The second sentence includes the starting and ending amounts along with the time frame, so it gives much more depth and weight to the accomplishment.

💡 *Aim to accept the right job, not just any job that takes you away from an employer you don't like.*

> **Stories from the Trenches...**
>
> One candidate emailed to check in: "I hope your wee is going well."

Employment

Examples of Employment Formatting
Here are a couple of sample employment sections to show you overall look.

A Sales Rep's resume

ABC Security Manufacturing   **Jun 2010 to Present**
Regional Sales Manager: May 2015 to Present
- Territory is GA, south AL, and north FL, and sell video, access control, and networking solutions, plus a suite of residential alarm products.
- On target to close $7.3M for 2019.
- **2015:** Earned *Record Breaker Award* for selling the most units in a month, plus the *President's Award*.
- **2016:** Earned *Record Breaker Award* for selling the most units in a month, plus the *President's Award*.

Commercial Sales Manager: Jan 2012 to May 2015
- Territory was GA, AL, and MS, and sold video, access control, and networking solutions.
- Called on dealers, distributors, VARs, and end users.
- Partnered with the Any Company team.
- Generated $5M in annual sales.
- **2013:** Ranked in the top 5 reps and earned the annual *President's Award*.
- **2014:** Ranked in the top 5, named *Top Manager* in the Southeast, and earned *President's Award*.

Video Sales Manager: Jun 2010 to Jan 2012.
- Territory was GA, AL, and MS, and sold a video suite of products to dealers, distributors, and end users.
- Generated $5M in annual sales.

An Operations Executive's resume

CDE Company   **Aug 2015 to Present**
General Manager
- Hold P/L for $200M and lead a team of 1000.
- Implemented LEAN globally, and conduct daily Gemba walks.
- Set up a visual management system at the central office to monitor all KPIs for 6 US plants, 3 international plants, and 1 fulfillment center.
- Saved $11M and increased EBITA by 11%.

EFG Company   **Sep 2010 to Jul 2015**
General Manager/VP of Operations
- Combined P/L for two divisions was $250M, and responsible for a global team of over 1000 across 5 plants.

JKL Company   **Jan 2000 to Apr 2010**
Plant Manager
- Held P/L of $88M and led a team of 350.
- Implemented a LEAN culture throughout plant and achieved over $4.5M in savings in the 1st 13 months.
- Reduced scrap from 27% to less than 9%, and improved EBITA by 19%.

Embrace failure. Without it, how can you know the full measure of success?

Employment

Let's do a compare and contrast. Here's page one of a résumé I received. A résumé writer had created this *functional* version for the candidate. It was a brutal read.

Robert (Bob) Smith
Vice President Global Operations

555-555-5555
email@email.com
Atlanta, GA

About Me

Award-winning and accomplished executive with proven record achieving quantifiable results delivering consistently profitable growth and technological innovation for manufacturing facilities and distribution centers in China, India, UK, Canada, and USA. Instrumental in streamlining organizational performance with total P&L responsibility, leading annual revenue of $150mm with twelve direct reports and twelve hundred indirect reports in nine facilities focusing on five distinct product families.

Skills

- Culture Building & Leadership
- Total Profit & Loss
- G&Os KIPs/Metrics
- Strategic & Tactical Planning, Implementation
- Budget Administration & Management
- Innovation/New Product Development
- Sales, Market & Channel Development
- Customer Service
- M&A Operational Due Diligence
- Contract Development & Negotiations
- Cost Reduction & Avoidance
- Inventory Control
- Logistics, Supply Chain & Distribution Networks
- Manufacturing Oversight
- Operational Process Redesign
- Market Analysis
- Purchase Management
- Recruiting & Staffing Initiatives
- Staff Development Programs
- Turnaround / Crisis Management

Profile

Accomplished in all phases of business development, administration & strategy, from controlling costs and maximizing revenues to harnessing team strengths to maximize performance. Built a career-long reputation as a transformational and passionate leader who relishes and meets the toughest challenges and is committed to furthering standards of excellence.

- Responsible for 12 direct reports plus 1,200 indirect staff across 9 manufacturing and distribution facilities for a $150mm business (ABC Company)
- Business Unit Manager/General Manager for a $35mm division with 14 direct reports (DEF Company)
- Operations Manager for a $100mm division with 9 direct reports, 200 indirect (GHI Company)
- Cultivated cultures conducive to productivity, high morale, and personal and team development
- Standardized manufacturing practices across all business units via best practices training
- Built a world-class supply chain/procurement team
- Delivered consistent cost reductions
- Expat status in Malaysia and India
- Implemented standardized metrics and KPIs across all business units and departments
- Optimized plants and distribution centers to reduce costs and build more efficient, highly adaptable supply chain and distribution
- Always sure to learn what is truly important to the buyer and end customers, implementing the changes that make us all but irreplaceable.

Select Highlights/Accomplishments
ABC Company

- Developed and led a world-class, high-performing operations team, and introduced my Six Core Principles and Training Models to instill best practices and create cross-divisional synergies company-wide
- Principles: 80/20 Quadrant Analysis (GHI Company), Procurement Excellence Metrics/Gemba, MRD (Kanban pull system and JIT), In-Lining, Process Flow Mapping
- Delivered $2.8mm annual savings from US operations, $800K from Asian operations by instilling procurement excellence and teaching the organization the best purchasing and negotiating skills
- Deployed the 80/20 model to support outsourcing decisions resulting in $1.4mm in savings and lower risk by converting $950K of fixed costs to variable
- Developed 2nd generation product, 7-figure sales to a major national club store
- Led operational due diligence and integration for two mergers.

Employment

This is the *chronological* version I created for him; it's much easier to see what was accomplished...and when.

Robert (Bob) Smith
Atlanta, GA · email@email.com · 555-555-5555

PROFESSIONAL SUMMARY

Award-winning and accomplished executive with a proven record of achieving quantifiable results and delivering consistently profitable growth and market driven innovation. Expertise in all phases of manufacturing, business development, administration & strategy. Experience running operations in the US, Canada, UK, China, and India. An expert in streamlining operations to maximize performance. Have held full P/L and have been responsible for business units up to $150M and teams of up to 1,200.
Full P/L · Operational Excellence · Innovation/New Product Development · Sales, Market & Channel Development
Customer Service · M&A Operational Due Diligence · Contract Development & Negotiation · Turnaround / Crisis Management

EXPERIENCE

ABC Company   **Apr 2014 to Feb 2020**
Manufacturer of safety products.
Vice President Global Operations & Supply Chain, Atlanta, GA. April 2014 to Feb 2020
- Responsible for a $150M business unit and led a team of 1,200 across 9 locations.
- Responsible for global demand fulfillment and managed Manufacturing, Safety, Distribution, Supply Chain, Quality, Material Management, Purchasing, Planning/Scheduling, Engineering, Customer Service, and HR.
- Standardized manufacturing practices and KPIs across all business units, and built a world-class procurement team.
- Reevaluated the make-vs-buy decision and identified more cost-effective sourcing.
- Introduced operational excellence practices including: 80/20 Quadrant Analysis, Procurement Excellence, Metrics/Gemba, MRD (Kanban pull system and JIT), In-Lining, and Value Stream Mapping
- Renegotiated purchasing agreements and saved $2.8M annually.
- Streamlined the manufacturing and distribution footprint and saved $1.4M.
- Converted $950K of fixed costs to variable.
- Developed the 2nd generation product and generated an additional $1.2M in revenue.
- Led the due diligence and integration of an acquired company into the ABC corporate environment.
- Consolidated a TN operation into an OH facility, saving $2M.
- Reduced direct labor US FTEs by 37%, and overseas FTEs by 8%.
- Evaluated strategic pricing and achieved a 12% increase in revenue across the core product set.
- Expanded the China campus by 25% in order to accommodate new product lines.
- Established and directed the India Sales and Distribution Center.

DEF Company   **Mar 2003 to Apr 2014**
Business Unit Manager (General Manager), Business Unit A, Atlanta, GA. March 2012 to April 2014
Manufacturer of metal components.
- Held P&L of $35M and led at team of 200 across 4 locations.
- Managed Sales, Customer Service, Marketing, Accounting, Manufacturing, Purchasing, Inventory, and Engineering.
- Tasked with streamlining the operation and deploying operational excellence throughout the business unit.
- Expanded the product offering from just 100% custom to include a standard product offering.
- Introduced 80/20 QuickShip which reduced lead-times from 8 weeks to 2 weeks.
- Transformed the revenue stream for 100% custom to 28% custom and 72% standard.
- Achieved 11% organic YOY revenue growth, and increased variable margin by 4% and gross margin by 6%.
- Achieved an 11-percentage-point improvement in Aftermarket customer satisfaction
- In 2012 and 2013, named to "Chicago's 101 Best and Brightest Companies to Work For."
- For Corporate, visited newly acquired companies to transition into the corporate family.
- Led the due diligence and integration of a newly acquired company into the DEF environment.

Operations & Supply Chain Manager, Business Unit B, Atlanta, GA, Mar 2009 to Mar 2012
Manufacturer of metal products.
- Directed Manufacturing, Purchasing, Inventory, Engineering, Customer Service, and Logistics.
- Established KPI Standards; the format then became accepted as Best Practices and used throughout sister divisions.

Education

A Litmus Test

The Education section is probably the section that's easiest to format, but it's where a lot of people trip up.

When reviewing a résumé for the first time, I ask every single candidate, "Is this education verifiable?" Most will say, "Of course!" But every now and then, someone will admit the degree/program/certification listed on the resume wasn't actually completed. This is a slippery slope you just don't want to go down because it's so easy to verify education these days, and if you're not truthful, you will be found out.

Case in point: I was conducting the initial phone screen with a CEO candidate and asked him if he'd completed the bachelor's degree he'd listed on his résumé. He said, "No, I didn't actually finish." I figured if he could justify lying about a degree, then what else had he embellished?

Another case in point: One candidate had just accepted an offer. He'd listed a degree on his application but admitted shortly thereafter that the degree hadn't actually been awarded. He'd finished all the coursework, but the university had withheld the degree due to an outstanding debt. He had made payments for a few years but stopped after being notified that additional coursework would now be required in order to meet new degree criteria. By claiming a degree he didn't have, he was fraudulent in the application process, so the offer was rescinded, even though he'd already resigned from his old job. A degree hadn't even been required for the new job in the first place, so if he'd just been honest about not having a degree, it wouldn't have even been a blip on the screen.

One more case in point for good measure, just in case I've not yet been clear enough: Another shoo-in candidate had run the gauntlet and received an offer. He'd listed an associate's degree on his résumé and application, but the background verification showed he hadn't actually finished the degree. It had been over sixteen years prior, and he couldn't remember what had happened. But here's the thing—when he ended his last class, he knew he didn't have the degree but at some point had started listing it on his résumé. This offer got rescinded, too, even though a degree hadn't been required for the job.

Bottom line? If you weren't awarded a certificate or degree, don't insinuate you have one.

Incomplete Education

If you're currently working on your degree, then use a phrase like *in progress* or *expected date of graduation*.
If you attended college but didn't finish the degree, then use *coursework towards a degree* or *didn't graduate*.

Not finishing your education program in no way reflects badly on you. Sometimes life just gets in the way, and you have to go in a different direction. What does make you look bad, though, is if you indicate you do have a degree when actually you do not.

> If you're a recent graduate, then you'll want to list your education at the top of your résumé. If you've been in the workforce for a while, then it can go to the bottom if it helps with spacing.

Stories from the Trenches...

One candidate described his middle management job as being "a piece of baloney in a sandwich...you get it from the top and the bottom."

Education

Formatting the Education Section

There are many ways to format this information, and here are some options.

EDUCATION

2009   High School Diploma, **West High School,** Jacksonville, FL.

An easy way to show education

EDUCATION

2013   BS Degree in Chemistry, **University of Anytown,** New York, NY
        Summa cum laude.

2009   High School Diploma, **West High School,** Anytown, NY
        GPA of 4.0.

Here, school honors are included

EDUCATION

2013   BS Degree in Chemistry, GPA of 3.90. **University of Anytown,** New York, NY
2009   HS Diploma, GPA of 4.0 and Valedictorian. **West High School,** Anytown, NY

This format saves space

EDUCATION

2018 to Present   **BS in Chemistry in progress,** University of Anytown, New York, NY.
                   Expected date of graduation, Spring 2022.

2009   **High School Diploma,** West High School, Anytown, NY

Using "in progress" or "expected date" makes it clear you've not yet finished the program.

EDUCATION

2012 to 2014   Worked towards an MS in Chemistry, **University of NY,** New York, NY.
2012   BS Degree in Chemistry, **University of Anytown,** St. Louis, MO.

This is how you can show coursework was started but not completed

EDUCATION

Worked towards an MS in Chemistry, **University of NY,** New York, NY   2012 to 2014
BS Degree in Chemistry, **University of Anytown,** St. Louis, MO.   2012

The date can be on the right if you prefer

💡 *If you look at the job search process in its entirety, it looks insurmountable. If you just concentrate on one step at a time, the daily process is much more manageable and the overall goal much more achievable.*

Education

A Couple More Samples of How to Efficiently Present Education

	EDUCATION	
1/2020 to Present	**Ph.D Candidate, Electrical and Computer Engineering; AB University,** Working on dissertation and scheduled to defend spring 2021.	
7/2018	**M.S., Control Theory and Engineering; CD University,** New York, NY **Thesis:** Pinky and the Brain; World domination in 3 Easy Steps.	
7/2014	**B.S, Automation; University of Anytown,** NY. GPA of 3.9 and graduated with Honors.	

Even if you have a lot of education, there's a way to list everything while still economizing on space.

EDUCATION

We can add in more detail to each education entry

University of NY, New York, NY. **Worked towards an MS in Chemistry.**   2012 to 2014
- GPA of 3.5 for coursework completed.

University of Anytown, St. Louis, MO. **BS Degree in Chemistry.**   2012
- GPA of 3.7.
- Completed 2 internships.
- Paid for 100% of education through part-time jobs and a work-study program.

You Paid Your Way

If you contributed to your education costs, then you are the exception and should *absolutely* put it on your résumé. Here's an example of how to list it. (Just use the percentage that's appropriate for you.)

EDUCATION

University of NY, New York, NY. **Worked towards an MS in Chemistry.**   2012 to 2014
- Paid 80% of tuition by working full time during university. GPA of 3.5 for coursework completed.

💡 To double-check that your employment and education dates make sense, ask someone to map out the path you've taken. If they can't track the route, then it needs a little reworking.

Stories from the Trenches...

My own worst typo: In 1987, while a secretary in a church, I was working on a special service bulletin. I should have typed, "The congregation will stand as the bread and wine are brought forward." Instead of "bread," I accidentally typed "break." Instead of "wine," I accidentally typed "wind."
So, yes, the congregation was to stand as the "break and wind" were brought forward.

Education

You Just Can't Make This Stuff Up
A sales manager had applied for a managerial role we had advertised online. One of the application questions was, "Have you completed the following level of education: Bachelor." He responded, "Yes."

> *[This is my email to the job seeker]*
>
> Hi ___,
> Thanks for your inquiry; unfortunately, the hiring president is requiring a Bachelor's degree and although you've listed 'yes' to the question, you have a notation on your resume that you didn't complete the degree. I'm so sorry, but this role isn't a match. I wish you all the best with your search!
> Cheers,
> Jane

> *[This is his reply back to me]*
>
> Jane,
> I appreciate your timely response. I also appreciate your policy in this regard. You will find that the widespread practice is to allow professional education and experience to "act as equivalent". As an actual adult educator, I have taught candidates with Master's/Ph.d credentials in all areas of the open market.
>
> Let us not forget my demonstrable and provable achievements as well.
>
> To simply not include me due to the letter of law would be...questionable. In order to find outstanding people we must be prepared to do outstanding things. This may include not standing on every piece of convention we see. Please forward my response to your President.
>
> Yours

This is a beautiful example of how *not* to be considered for future job opportunities.

Sometimes Sassy Does Work
A candidate was interviewing with a medical device company. Even though he had no degree, the team had him drive all over creation to interview. In the final meeting, the interviewer said, "I can't believe you've gotten this far since you don't have a degree." The candidate acknowledged that, then said, "I understand you don't have a degree either, sir, so how did you get your job? All I want is a chance, and I know I'm a diamond in the rough." He got the job offer that day.

What made the biggest difference here is that the candidate wasn't at all arrogant or condescending. He had done his homework on the interviewer and was quietly confident when he delivered that humdinger of a closing question.

> 💡 On your résumé, use the term bachelor or bachelor's, not baccalaureate. No one's going to search for the word baccalaureate.

> **Stories from the Trenches...**
>
> I joked to a candidate that I wanted to be Queen of Recruiting. He said he'd be more impressed if my title were Queen of Placements because it's not about function, it's about results.
>
> A most excellent point.

Spacing

Page Breaks

To avoid confusion, aim for a nice clean page break.

In this example, Bob didn't have enough room on page one to list all his 2012 to 2015 accomplishments, so he continued on the next page and put *Achievements continued…* at the top of the second page.

Robert (Bob) Smith
Address • Email Address • Phone

Education

BS Degree, Anytown University.   **1990**

Employment History

ABC Security Integration   **Jun 2010 to Present**
Regional Sales Manager: May 2015 to Present
- Territory is GA, south AL, and north FL, and sell video, access control, and networking solutions, plus a suite of residential alarm products.
- On target to close $7.3M for 2019.
- **2015:** Earned President's Award, and *Record Breaker Award* for selling the most units in a month.
- **2016:** Earned *Record Breaker Award* for selling the most units in a month, plus the *President's Award*.

Commercial Sales Manager: Jan 2012 to May 2015.
- Territory was GA, AL, and MS, and sold video, access control, and networking solutions.
- Called on dealers, distributors, VARs, and end users.
- Generated $5M in annual sales.
- **2013:** Ranked in the top 5 reps in Atlanta, and earned the *President's Award*.

Achievements continued…

- **2014:** Ranked in the top 5 reps in Atlanta, named *Top Manager* in the Southeast, and earned the *President's Award*.

Video Sales Manager: Jun 2010 to Jan 2012.
- Territory was GA, AL, and MS, and sold a video suite of products to dealers, distributors, and end users.
- Generated $5M in annual sales.

It's not very tidy, though, and gives it a choppy feel.

Stories from the Trenches…

I was conducting a search for an entry-level consultant and had a scheduled 9:30 a.m. call with a candidate. He answered the phone with a very sleepy, "Hello?" I told him I was calling for our scheduled conversation, and he said, "Well, it appears I'm catching up on my sleep." I asked him to call back when he had time, then scratched his name off my list. Well, he called back a few hours later and apologized for the way he'd answered the phone. He explained he'd had to work until 1:30 a.m. to close out two sales. He was a car salesman, and a customer had walked in midevening to look at cars, and it had taken until 9:00 p.m. to finish the paperwork. Another customer had seen the lights on and walked into the showroom, too, and he ended up buying a car as well. This candidate had only been on the job for a few weeks, so these were his first sales. He turned out to be a great young man and just needed a break in his luck.

The moral of this story is that if you trip up, it's not the end of the world. Just be professional, extend a genuine apology for your behavior, and cross your fingers. If the person to whom you're apologizing can't get over the incident, then you're better off without them.

Spacing

To achieve a clean page break, I moved the Education section to the second page, which improved the flow.

Robert (Bob) Smith
Address · Email Address · Phone

Employment History

ABC Security Integration   Jun 2010 to Present
Regional Sales Manager: May 2015 to Present
- Territory is GA, south AL, and north FL, and sell video, access control, and networking solutions, plus a suite of residential alarm products.
- On target to close $7.3M for 2019.
- **2015:** Earned President's Award, and *Record Breaker Award* for selling the most units in a month.
- **2016:** Earned *Record Breaker Award* for selling the most units in a month, plus the *President's Award*.

Commercial Sales Manager: Jan 2012 to May 2015.
- Territory was GA, AL, and MS, and sold video, access control, and networking solutions.
- Called on dealers, distributors, VARs, and end users.
- Generated $5M in annual sales.
- **2013:** Ranked in the top 5 reps in Atlanta, and earned the *President's Award.*
- **2014:** Ranked in the top 5 reps in Atlanta, named *Top Manager* in the Southeast, and earned the *President's Award.*

Video Sales Manager: Jun 2010 to Jan 2012.
- Territory was GA, AL, and MS, and sold a video suite of products to dealers, distributors, and end users.
- Generated $5M in annual sales.

Education

BS Degree, Anytown University.   1990

Digits versus Writing Out the Number

Formal writing rules are a bit relaxed when it comes to the résumé so, instead of writing out a number or a percentage in full, we can use digits instead. It's a great space-saving trick and here's an example.

- Led a team of twelve direct reports and a down-line team of twenty-five, which represented fifty percent of the operation.
- Led a team of 12 direct reports and a down-line team of 25, which represented 50% of the operation.

Whichever form you use, just make sure you're consistent throughout your résumé.

> The best order in which to list information is to start with those skills and experience that are primary, then list everything else in order of importance.

Stories from the Trenches...

An executive wasn't a match for a general manager role because he didn't have a bachelor's degree. He yelled, "Amazing that college twenty-five years ago is more important than a successful career! Probably not a good fit!" Then said very sweetly, "Please keep me in mind for future opportunities."

Spacing

No Set Rule

There's no requirement regarding which sections should go where. As long as your contact information is at the very top, you can do whatever you want. To figure out what works best, just put everything into the document and then massage the spacing until you get a tidy look with clean page breaks.

Here, Bob has Education and Patents at the bottom of the résumé...

Robert (Bob) Smith
New York, NY • bob@email.com • 555-555-5555

SUMMARY

- Detail, detail, detail, detail, detail, detail, detail, detail.
- Detail, detail, detail, detail, detail, detail, detail, detail, detail.
- Detail, detail, detail, detail, detail, detail, detail.
- Detail, detail, detail, detail, detail, detail, detail, detail, detail.
- Detail, detail, detail, detail, detail, detail, detail.
- Detail, detail, detail, detail, detail, detail, detail, detail.

EMPLOYMENT

Jan 2010 to Present   **Principal Engineer, ABC Company,** Anytown, NY
- Detail, detail, detail, detail, detail, detail, detail.
- Detail, detail, detail, detail, detail, detail, detail, detail, detail.
- Detail, detail, detail, detail, detail, detail, detail, detail, detail, detail, detail,
- Detail, detail, detail, detail, detail, detail, detail.
- Detail, detail, detail, detail, detail, detail, detail, detail, detail, detail, detail, detail.
- Detail, detail, detail, detail, detail, detail, detail.
- Detail, detail, detail, detail, detail, detail, detail, detail.
- Detail, detail, detail, detail, detail, detail, detail.

Jan 2007 to Dec 2009   **Senior Engineer, JKL Company,** Anytown, NY
- Detail, detail, detail, detail, detail, detail, detail, detail.
- Detail, detail, detail, detail, detail, detail, detail.
- Detail, detail, detail, detail, detail, detail, detail, detail, detail.

Apr 1995 to Nov 2006   **Principal Engineer, RST Company,** Anytown, NY
- Detail, detail, detail, detail, detail, detail, detail.
- Detail, detail, detail, detail, detail, detail, detail, detail, detail, detail, detail, detail, detail, detail, detail.

PATENTS ←

US Patent 1111111: "Name of patent".
US Patent 2222222: "Name of patent".

EDUCATION ←

BSEE, Rensselaer Polytechnic Institute, Troy, NY.

💡 List *all* your work history, even if you completely changed industries. That seemingly unrelated experience demonstrates your ability to adapt.

Stories from the Trenches...

A candidate apologized for a late response, so I told him it was totally OK, and although I wanted to be the center of the universe, I didn't think anyone had gotten that memo. My company name is Northstar, so he said, "Well, you're only magnetic north...not true north." Well played, my friend, well played.

Spacing

...but they absolutely can be moved closer to the top to put more emphasis on them.

Robert (Bob) Smith
New York, NY • bob@email.com • 555-555-5555

EDUCATION

BSEE, Rensselaer Polytechnic Institute (RPI), Troy, NY.

SUMMARY

- Detail, detail, detail, detail, detail, detail, detail, detail.
- Detail, detail, detail, detail, detail, detail, detail, detail, detail, detail.
- Detail, detail, detail, detail, detail, detail, detail.
- Detail, detail, detail, detail, detail, detail, detail, detail, detail.
- Detail, detail, detail, detail, detail, detail, detail.
- Detail, detail, detail, detail, detail, detail, detail, detail, detail, detail.

PATENTS

US Patent 1111111: "Name of patent".
US Patent 2222222: "Name of patent".

EMPLOYMENT

Jan 2010 to Present   **Principal Engineer, ABC Company,** Anytown, NY
- Detail, detail, detail, detail, detail, detail, detail.
- Detail, detail, detail, detail, detail, detail, detail, detail, detail.
- Detail, detail, detail, detail, detail, detail, detail, detail, detail, detail, detail,
- Detail, detail, detail, detail, detail, detail, detail.
- Detail, detail, detail, detail, detail, detail, detail, detail, detail, detail, detail, detail.
- Detail, detail, detail, detail, detail, detail, detail.
- Detail, detail, detail, detail, detail, detail, detail, detail, detail.
- Detail, detail, detail, detail, detail, detail, detail.

Jan 2007 to Dec 2009   **Senior Engineer, JKL Company,** Anytown, NY
- Detail, detail, detail, detail, detail, detail, detail, detail, detail.
- Detail, detail, detail, detail, detail, detail, detail.
- Detail, detail, detail, detail, detail, detail, detail, detail, detail.

Apr 1995 to Nov 2006   **Principal Engineer, RST Company,** Anytown, NY
- Detail, detail, detail, detail, detail, detail, detail.
- Detail, detail, detail, detail, detail, detail, detail, detail, detail, detail, detail, detail, detail, detail, detail.

Is Spacing Important?

Using sensible and consistent spacing is the key to giving your résumé that polished, uniform look that signals to the reader you're detail oriented and professional.

> While there is room to be creative, don't go wild. You might be avant-garde in your thinking, but the reader may not be. The goal, then, is to find that fine line between highlighting your personality while still demonstrating a high level of professionalism.

Stories from the Trenches...

A candidate explained his reason for interest in a role: "It would get me out of my work-release days."

Spacing

Spacing Tricks

The biggest complaint I hear from candidates is they can't fit all the information onto two pages. With a few spacing adjustments, though, we can actually free up a lot of real estate on the page. In the example below, Bob's maxed out on space and will need a third page if he wants to add anything extra to his résumé

Robert Smith
Address
Email Address, Phone

Professional Summary

- Seasoned sales representative in the healthcare sector.
- Primary focus on small and medium regional hospitals.
- Call on Facilities Managers and C-Level executives.
- Sell physical and logical security solutions.
- Products include Access Control, CCTV, IP Video, Surveillance, Readers, Biometrics, and ID Management.
- Carry a quota of $2M and have exceeded quota 8 out of the last 10 years.
- Awarded President's Club 7 consecutive years from 2006 to 2012.

Employment History

ABC Company   **Jun 2010 to Present**

Regional Sales Manager: May 2015 to Present

- Territory is GA, south AL, and north FL, and sell video, access control, and networking solutions, plus a suite of residential alarm products.

Achievements continued

- On target to close $7.3M for 2019.
- **2015:** Earned President's Award, and *Record Breaker Award* for selling the most units in a month.
- **2016:** Earned *Record Breaker Award* for selling the most units in a month, plus *President's Award*.

Commercial Sales Manager: Jan 2012 to May 2015

- Territory was GA, AL, and MS, and sold video, access control, and networking solutions.
- Called on dealers, distributors, VARs, and end users.
- Generated $5M in annual sales.
- **2013:** Ranked in the top 5 reps in Atlanta, and earned the *President's Award*.
- **2014:** Ranked in the top 5 reps in Atlanta, named *Top Manager* in the Southeast, and earned the *President's Award*.

Video Sales Manager: Jun 2010 to Jan 2012

- Territory was GA, AL, and MS, and sold a video suite of products to dealers, distributors, and end users.
  Generated $5M in annual sales.

Education

BS Degree, Anytown University.   1990

By narrowing margins, slightly reducing the font, eliminating spare lines between titles and bullets, and combining contact information onto a single line, we can free up an additional half page. Double points!

Robert Smith
Address • Email Address • Phone

Education
BS Degree, Anytown University.   1990

Professional Summary

- Seasoned sales representative in the healthcare sector.
- Primary focus on small and medium regional hospitals.
- Call on Facilities Managers and C-Level executives.
- Sell physical and logical security solutions.
- Products include Access Control, CCTV, IP Video, Surveillance, Readers, Biometrics, and ID
- Carry a quota of $2M and have exceeded quota 8 out of the last 10 years.
- Awarded President's Club 7 consecutive years from 2006 to 2012.

Employment History

ABC Company   **Jun 2010 to Present**
Regional Sales Manager: May 2015 to Present

- Territory is GA, south AL, and north FL, and sell video, access control, and networking solutions, plus a suite of residential alarm products.
- On target to close $7.3M for 2019.
- **2015:** Earned President's Award, and *Record Breaker Award* for selling the most units in a month.
- **2016:** Earned *Record Breaker Award* for selling the most units in a month, plus the *President's Award*.

Commercial Sales Manager: Jan 2012 to May 2015.

- Territory was GA, AL, and MS, and sold video, access control, and networking solutions.
- Called on dealers, distributors, VARs, and end users.
- Generated $5M in annual sales.
- **2013:** Ranked in the top 5 reps in Atlanta, and earned the *President's Award*.
- **2014:** Ranked in the top 5 reps in Atlanta, named *Top Manager* in the Southeast, and earned the *President's Award*.

Video Sales Manager: Jun 2010 to Jan 2012

- Territory was GA, AL, and MS, and sold a video suite of products to dealers, distributors, and end users.
- Generated $5M in annual sales.

Page Naming

Don't Name Your Pages

When the world was driven by paper, your name and page number had to be on the top of every page because that was the only way to put the résumé back in order if the staple or paper clip came loose. These days your résumé may never even be printed out, so page naming is now just a waste of space.

Also, page naming can actually create a formatting problem. In this example, Bob's page name was at the top of page two, but it got pushed farther down the page when I made a spacing change on page one.

Robert (Bob) Smith
Anytown, NY
bob@email.com
555-555-5555

Employment History

ABC Security Integration   Jun 2010 to Present
Regional Sales Manager: May 2015 to Present
- Territory is GA, south AL, and north FL, and sell video, access control, and networking solutions, plus a suite of residential alarm products.
- On target to close $7.3M for 2019.
- **2015:** Earned President's Award, and *Record Breaker Award* for selling the most units in a month.
- **2016:** Earned *Record Breaker Award* for selling the most units in a month, plus the *President's Award*.

Commercial Sales Manager: Jan 2012 to May 2015.
- Territory was GA, AL, and MS, and sold video, access control, and networking solutions.
- Called on dealers, distributors, VARs, and end users.
- Generated $5M in annual sales.
- **2013:** Ranked in the top 5 reps in Atlanta, and earned the *President's Award*.

- **2014:** Ranked in the top 5 reps in Atlanta, named *Top Manager* in the Southeast, and earned the *President's Award*.

Bob Smith, bob@email.com • 555-555-5555   Page 2

Video Sales Manager: Jun 2010 to Jan 2012.
- Territory was GA, AL, and MS, and sold a video suite of products to dealers, distributors, and end users.
- Generated $5M in annual sales.

Education

BS Degree, Anytown University.   1990

Don't put the page name or number in the header, either, because you just never know if the database will read it or not.

Just forget about naming or counting pages, and use the space for more important information instead.

Font size isn't nearly as important as it used to be. When résumés were printed out and snail mailed to a company, the font had to be such that the reader didn't need a magnifying glass to read it. Now that résumés are emailed, the font can be a little smaller, since the reader can expand the document size on the screen if needed.

Stories from the Trenches...

An introductory note from a candidate to a colleague who needed help with a job search: "There are recruiters, and then there is Jane...she's like Yoda except she's taller, way better looking, and not green."

References

Your References

Space is at a premium on a résumé, so listing the phrase "References available upon request" takes up valuable real estate. Since it's highly unlikely a company will hire you if you refuse to provide references, leave off this phrase, and use the space for more substantive information.

Here's a to-do list for when you do provide reference information.

- Have a list of references in a separate document. Get permission from each person to include them on the list, and then alert them to a potential call to make sure they're not surprised.
- Make sure each reference's contact information is current.
- Make sure you list people who'll be complimentary of your work.
- Do *not* list your references' names on your résumé, because an unethical recruiter might use that information as a springboard into additional recruiting conversations. You do not want to end up competing with one of your peer references for a job you saw first.

What Information to Provide

In your reference list, include your reference's name, title, company, and how you know them.

> **Robert M. Smith**
> 555-123-1234 • rsmith@domain.com
>
> **REFERENCES**
>
> **Sam Smith, VP of Sales,** ABC Company
> 555-555-5555, samsmith@abcco.com
> Relationship: Sam hired me to work at ABC Company in 1997, and I worked for him for 15 years.
>
> **Judy Jones, President/CEO,** XYZ Company
> 444-444-4444, judyj@xyzco.com
> Relationship: Judy owns XYZ and has been a customer of mine for the last 10 years.
>
> **Phil Brown,** JKL Distributors
> 333-333-3333, phil.brown@jkl.com
> Relationship: Phil worked for me when I was the Sales Manager at ABC.

A sample reference list

💡 **Save regularly, spend wisely, argue fairly, and apologize sincerely.**

Stories from the Trenches...

An interviewer asked a candidate, "What's your biggest weakness?" There was a really long pause, then the candidate said, "Apparently, it's thinking on my feet."

General Tips for Résumés

Write for the End Audience
You know your expertise, your company, and your industry, but a recruiter may not, so gear your résumé to the reader who's the least educated about what you do. I'm not saying to dumb it down; just write plainly and succinctly, and make it easy for a newbie to follow the responsibilities you've held and the path you've taken.

Spell-Check and Grammar-Check
I'm a bit of a grammar nut, so I suppose I could take a moment to talk about dangling participles and split infinitives, but I never mastered diagramming in high school and still think of a dangling participle as something that likely needs medical attention. Healthcare issues aside, though, make sure your writing is grammatically correct and flows easily.

Reading your résumé aloud will help identify any grammatical errors. Some things to double-check:

- Is your current role written in present tense?
- Are your previous job details in past tense?
- Do your subjects and verbs agree?
- Are your possessive apostrophes in the right place?
- Have you avoided ending sentences with prepositions?
- Do all the sections consistently line up across the ruler (centered, left justified, right justified)?

If you're not sure about the correct grammar, Grammarly.com has great information.

Proofread, Proofread, Proofread!
You've read your résumé a hundred times over and haven't caught any errors over the last five passes, so you give it to someone else to proof, and they find five errors in the first paragraph. How can that be? The issue is you've read the words so many times you've become numb to them. Your brain knew what was coming next, so your eyes just skimmed over the words, instead of reading them.

To overcome this, print out your résumé, and read it in reverse from the bottom of the last page to the top of the first page. Read it line by line, bullet by bullet, and use a ruler to guide your eyes. The words will now be fresh, and you'll catch errors you've repeatedly missed.

Submitting in PDF or Word
If a recruiter can't convert your PDF résumé to Word, then your résumé has to be cut and pasted from PDF into a new Word document, which can wreak havoc with the formatting. If this happens, the new Word version that gets saved to the database may not look as you intended. It's just best to send both Word and PDF versions and let the recruiter choose whichever version is compatible with the database.

Winston Churchill said, "If you're going through hell, keep going."

Stories from the Trenches…

One candidate in a high-visibility role described himself as having "…the ability to work in a high virility role."

General Tips for Résumés

Do Not Password Protect
Do not password protect your résumé. If it is protected, then a recruiter won't be able to upload it to the database and will have to email you back and ask for an unprotected copy. If you want someone to consider your résumé, then don't password protect it.

A Suggestion Going Forward
We think we'll remember everything but, in reality, details fade over time. To avoid this, create a recurring quarterly, semi-annual, or annual *personal* calendar entry reminding you to add recent accomplishments to your résumé. Another option is to create a folder in Outlook and just email yourself a note about any new accomplishments. Whatever the method, just store information away on a regular basis; then you'll have all the details ready to go when you want to update your résumé.

Case in point: A sales rep was asked to meet her boss at the local airport and was told to bring her laptop. No sooner had she sat down with him than he told her he was "going in another direction" and took her laptop. In an instant, she was unemployed. All her sales achievements were on that confiscated computer, so updating her résumé became a guessing game.

Newfangled Fads
Of late, I've seen people include a visual representation of skills, but it's a poor use of space and not really of much use to a recruiter.

This is how one individual represented his skills on his résumé, but he didn't do himself any favors because he indicated that while he was good at public speaking, problem-solving, persevering, and working on a team, his product knowledge and communication skills were less than excellent.

Presentation & Public Speaking	√ √ √ √ √
Creativity & Problem Solving	√ √ √ √
Perseverance	√ √ √ √
Teamwork	√ √ √ √
Product Knowledge	√ √ √
Written & Oral Communication	√ √ √

Instead of a pictorial, use the space to list responsibilities and achievements; then those characteristics you want to highlight will naturally shine through.

> To be a leader, you need people to follow you. Robin Hood could run around the forest blazing a trail all day long, but unless the posse followed him, he was just a creepy guy skulking in the trees.

Stories from the Trenches...

A job seeker wanted to assure me that his former employer would speak well of him, so he emailed me saying, "they'll give me a glaring reference."

Another job seeker claimed he, "built customer intimacy."

General Tips for Résumés

Your Picture on Your Résumé
In Europe, it's commonplace for a headshot to be on the résumé. In the United States, however, not so much. From a formatting perspective, it's one more thing that can corrupt the database upload process. From a judgment perspective, it can make the job seeker look less than ideal if the picture isn't particularly professional.

It's best to leave it off and just have a picture on your LinkedIn profile instead.

Customizing for Each Résumé Submission
It's natural to want to customize your résumé for each job submission, but going that route means you'll end up having to say to a recruiter, "I don't know which résumé version you have." The recruiter will then naturally assume you've enhanced experience to meet what you *think* is needed, instead of just being accurate.

The best approach is to create one master résumé that genuinely reflects your experience, and let it go at that. For sure, a recruiter might ask for a specific change, and you should oblige and provide what's requested. If that change makes sense overall, include it in your master copy. Just don't customize your résumé for every job submission. You'll drive yourself crazy trying to second-guess the requirements.

Once the Résumé Is Complete
Once you're happy with your updated résumé, consider deleting all the other copies in order to avoid submitting an old version. If you can't bear to part with the old versions, move them to a separate folder so they're off your radar screen.

If You Are Tempted to "Enhance" Your Résumé
If you do puff up your résumé, at some point your lack of experience will become apparent, and you won't be able to handle a situation that would be a no-brainer if you actually had the experience you claim. If you're always accurate, you will never get caught unawares.

Just Let It Be
If you've not gotten the expected responses to your résumé submissions, there might be a tendency to blame the résumé and then to start changing it. Out of frustration, you might even throw in the towel on the old version and start from scratch using a newfangled template or column format. But just stop a moment and take a breather.

If you feel your résumé is an accurate reflection of you, and you really like the finished product, then leave it alone, and just concentrate on submitting your résumé for more jobs. Callbacks will come. Just give it time, and don't give up.

If you're going to be a successful leader, you're going to need a backbone.

Stories from the Trenches...

Reason for leaving a job was a "market shift." Unfortunately, the *f* was left off.

Cover Letters

The Dreaded Cover Letter

People hate writing cover letters, and people hate reading them. In the past, the cover letter was the primary way to gauge a person's writing skills, but these days, the cover letter can be written by the actual sender or a résumé writer, or it can just be a cut-and-paste job from the internet, so it's no longer an accurate measure.

The issue with a generic cover is that it's too easy to forget to change the recipient's name. If you send a letter to *Hello{Name}*, you just look careless.

If the application instructions say to provide a cover, then include one. If the instructions don't mention it, then don't bother with one.

What to Cover in the Cover

Include any information requested, but keep the whole thing short and sweet. The less you say, the better. Here are some examples.

> Dear___
> Attached is my resume in response to the Director of Sales listing you have on LinkedIn. I meet all the criteria and would welcome the chance to be considered if you feel my background is a good match.
> Thank you for your time and consideration.

> Dear___
> I've been referred to you by a colleague who sent me your LinkedIn listing for a Director of Sales, and attached is my resume for your review. I meet all the criteria except for having 10 years of sales leadership instead of 12 years. If there's flexibility in the requirements, I'd welcome the chance to be considered if you feel my background is a good fit.
> Thank you for your time and consideration.

If you don't meet the criteria and mention that in the cover letter, you'll come across as humble and well grounded.

> Dear___
> I saw your listing for a Director of Sales on LinkedIn, and attached is my resume for your review. The listing requires that candidates live in Georgia and I'm very willing to relocate if that would be an option. If not, I'd welcome the chance to be considered for any other opportunities in the future.
> Thank you for your time and consideration.

If you're cutting and pasting contact information into a cover letter, make sure the newly added font matches what's already written. Proofreading is critical, so use the same editing techniques for the cover as you did for your résumé

> **Stories from the Trenches...**
>
> A candidate said, "So many people have changed my résumé, I've lost my way."

Cover Letters

Carelessness Could Be a Calamity
Here's a cover letter I received.

> **Robert (Bob) Smith**
> **Anytown, NY • bob@email.com • 555-555-5555**
>
> Date
>
> Company Representative
> Title Company Name
> Company Address
> City, State, Zip
>
> Dear Company Representative:
>
> As a National Account Manager for a computer company with industry status as a top 50 systems builder…..

The job seeker completely failed to customize the cover letter in any way, shape, or form. I opened this up, laughed out loud, then printed it out and tossed it in my save-it-for-the-book file.

A Quick Reminder
Remember the rule about making sure your contact information is at the top of the page? The same rule also applies for your cover letter.

This job seeker sent a single document with his cover letter being on page one and his résumé on pages two and three. He hadn't listed any contact information at the top of his cover letter, so his name in the database, quite bizarrely, ended up being *Toronto September Th*.

> Toronto, September 11th, 2014
>
> North star Recruiting
> Attention; Jane Snipes
>
> Re: Opportunity VP of Sales
>
> Ms. Snipes

Name	Th, Toronto September
Address 1	

This is how he showed up in the database

> 💡 When texting, type out every word. Don't use "yeah" for "yes", and don't use text shortcuts. Do limit the use of emojis.

Stories from the Trenches…

A sales rep's review of his former boss: "Maybe the anti-Christ needs a job and can work with him."

Cover Letters

Be Persnickety with Your Wording
You can have the most brilliantly written résumé, but if you send in a cover letter with grammar and spelling errors, then you've just demonstrated a lack of attention to detail.

Here's a cover letter I received from a college senior.

> Hello Ms. Jane! Im graduating in may and i am an English major. I know now is the time to star send in out résumé to job but ive never had to write a résumé and i only had one summer job at goodwill. Im extremely nervous that i wont be able to get a job after graduation. Is there anyway you could help me with this résuméproblem?

Hold yourself to a high standard, and be vigilant about your grammar and spelling.

An Awesome Cover Letter
In 2016, I received this cover letter in response to a job I'd listed on LinkedIn.

> Thank you for your time, I hope you are doing well. In early 2015 my company announced a retail channel exit strategy by the end of 2015. Myself and others were laid off before the Thanksgiving holiday due to the retail exit strategy. I am hopeful that my 17 years of experience working within national account sales, successful history growing national account portfolios, my knowledge of the retail channel, and work experience managing diverse work groups would be assets related to my search.
>
> In my search, I came across the Director of Sales role you have posted on LinkedIn. Unfortunately, the posting is closed for new submissions so I've attached my personal resume. Is it too late to submit for the role?
>
> I truly appreciate your time, have a great evening.

The candidate gave a fast overview of his expertise, then acknowledged that the job posting had already closed out. It was an excellent approach, and he was firing on all cylinders in his introduction.

Don't Be Repetitive
Your well-composed résumé has all the information needed, so don't reiterate your entire career in your cover letter.

Read the job description, and identify a couple of the primary requirements, then touch on those briefly in the cover letter. If you write *War and Peace,* you'll come across as verbose, and no one will read it.

> If you tend to talk too much, put a note on your desk that says, "Stop talking!" I've had one taped to my screen for fifteen years. It's very faded, but it's mostly done the trick.

Stories from the Trenches…

A candidate attempting to reiterate his interest in a role: "I wanted to Putney self forward." Autocorrect…can't live with it and can't live without it.

Why Are You Searching?

Why Are You Looking for a New Job?

Are you a new college graduate? Or were you pushed out of your last role due to a reduction in force? Or are you in a job you just don't like and are ready to change?

New Graduate: Just know that your first job doesn't define you. It's just a single step in a journey of ten thousand steps.

Casualty of a Downsizing, Rightsizing, or Seasonal Correction: Sometimes it's politics; sometimes it's just bad luck. Whatever the reason, just know you are not alone. The situation is fixable, and although your next role may not be your dream job, you *will* find a job.

Currently Employed but Really Want to Be Somewhere Else: If you spend most of your waking hours dreaming of winning the lottery and telling your boss to take a long walk off a short pier, there is a way to navigate out of where you are.

Reverse Engineering Can Be Invaluable

Most people fall into their career accidentally. They took a job early on because they had bills to pay; then that job took on a mind of its own and turned into a career.

Whether you're just starting out or you want to reinvent yourself, one of the best ways to figure out what's possible is to look on LinkedIn at the profiles of those who are already doing the job you'd like to have. Check out the career path each person took to get into that role. Do you need additional education or training to get there? How long would it take to achieve, and how much would it cost? Is that a path feasible from where you are now? Is it a path you even want to undertake?

If you only look forward to where you want to be, the way can be too hazy. If you picture yourself in your chosen role, and then look back at the path needed to get there, you can better decide if it's a good option for you.

Here's Where an Objective Can Help

We don't really want to list an objective on your résumé because it might get your résumé sidelined if the screener doesn't perceive the vacancy matches the goal you've listed. But by taking time to put your ideal job down on a separate piece of paper, you can sharpen your own vision of the direction you'd like to take—plus, you'll have a nice benchmark against which you can compare and contrast new opportunities as they surface. As you go through the interview process, you can eliminate opportunities that don't match your objective.

Can you empty a swimming pool? Yes, you can. It just takes a bit of time and a really good bucket.

> **Stories from the Trenches...**
>
> A senior HR executive was leading a video panel interview. When the candidate joined the video, the team saw an unmade bed in the background...and what appeared to be a body buried under all the blankets. The HR exec said if you stared at that bedding long enough, you swore it moved! To make things *even more* interesting, the candidate appeared to be getting interview answers from the bedding heap. To top it off, the bedroom's décor was 1970s rock memorabilia, and the candidate wrapped up the interview with a ten-minute dissertation about his favorite rock band.

Managing the Roller Coaster of Emotions

You Just Can't Breathe
There might be moments during the search when you feel like you're either paralyzed or drowning. It's only natural for emotions to run high, and you can go from being numb to depressed to angry to hopeful, then back to numb again. These emotions can hit all at once, or you can bounce from one to another with lightning speed. This cycle is *totally* normal, and it's all part of the process.

If Only
Regret is the greatest pain there is. One small decision can send you off in an unintended direction and put you far from your desired destination, but that doesn't mean you can't map out a new course to get back on track. You are *never* stuck. If you're not where you want to be right now, don't panic. Just think through your options, look realistically at all the consequences, and choose the path that will yield the *least* amount of regret down the road. Be brave; be bold. It's all going to be okay.

Don't Look Back
Continuing to feel shame over a decision you've made is fruitless and exhausting—plus, it makes you procrastinate because you're afraid to make yet another mistake.

Case in point: A candidate was ashamed for not having finished his degree almost twenty years prior. His choices back then had been to continue with college or to take a job with a super company. He'd chosen employment and had moved up the ranks quickly. Later on, he joined a start-up, which he helped put on the map. Even though he'd been incredibly successful, he still felt major regret over not having finished his degree and was afraid it would be held against him, so he put off updating his résumé for months. To get unstuck, he made a list of all his accomplishments, which gave him a fresh view of his success and was just the boost he needed to update his résumé.

Fear of failure makes you procrastinate, but the only way you really fail is if you don't try. So just give it a go, play full out, and don't leave anything on the table.

Is It Okay to Have a Pity Party?
Absolutely! Everybody needs a good pout and a pity party every now and then, but put a time limit on it…an hour, half a day, maybe a day. Just keep it short, and don't let that bad mood bleed into your job-search time.

The best way to vaporize self-pity is gratitude. Are you above ground? Yes? Great! You have the power to change your circumstances. Have a good wallow for a few minutes, then pick yourself up, dust yourself off, and get moving.

Take Your Own Advice
When you're in a tough spot, pretend you're providing counsel to someone who has the exact same situation as you. What's your advice? If it resembles anything like "Stop whining and get going," then take your own advice.

> Healing doesn't mean the damage never existed; it just means the damage no longer has control over your life.

Stories from the Trenches…

Seen on a LinkedIn: "I used to be good. Now I'm just retired and cheap."

Managing the Roller Coaster of Emotions

22 and 212: Great numbers to consider (two great books to read)
In *212: The Extra Degree,* Sam Parker and Mac Anderson drive home the fact that, at 211 degrees, water is just hot. Adding a single degree of heat changed the world.

In *When They Were 22,* Brad Dunn highlights how difficult situations can be a springboard into fantastic opportunities.

Both books are eye-openers!

Just Be Nice
It doesn't matter how badly your employer treated you. You must be cordial, pleasant, controlled, measured, nice, kind, polite, civil, and appreciative in every single conversation. Even if the information being told to you isn't what you want to hear, having a positive attitude will show maturity and self-control.

Learning to Cope with Bad News
We're never taught how to deliver bad news, so when someone has to deliver it, there's a tendency for them to become distant, curt, and cold. It's a self-defense mechanism used to get through the conversation.

If you're getting terminated, you want your boss to be empathetic and compassionate—and to remember the loyalty you've demonstrated and the contribution you've made—but instead, he or she is devoid of emotion and just wants to get the conversation over with. Even those you've trusted and admired can fail you miserably, and the pain from what was said can rattle around in your brain for a long time and be so much more painful than the job loss ever was in the first place.

Sometimes bad news comes in the form of silence. You've sent your résumé to fifty companies, but not gotten a single reply. Maybe you've nailed the on-site interview and were told you'd hear back in two days, but that was two weeks ago. The silence can be soul crushing. It might feel like you're living in the bend in the toilet, but there *is* a job out there for you, and you are not alone. Just stick to your daily routine, and don't give up.

Deciding on a Fork in the Road before You've Even Left Home
A common question from candidates is how to limit the search in order to help to control the chaos that is a natural part of any job search. Until a job offer is on the table, however, there's really no decision to be made, so go broad, go deep, and go wide with your search, and look at any and every possibility within the general scope of your skills and expertise. By drawing a wide circle, you'll gain interviewing experience and insight into jobs you might not have considered before, plus the compare and contrast between opportunities will help you crystallize the best option for you. Be welcoming of any and all conversations, and run multiple searches in parallel until you land a new job.

> Anger is sadness you have refused to process.

Stories from the Trenches...

I'd let an applicant know he wasn't qualified for a role, so he emailed me at 2:00 a.m. saying, "Why don't you go back to your home country, where they have bad teeth and poor hair."

On the other hand, someone called me his "telephone barstool buddy," and yet another called me a "wordsmith samurai"...so the feedback all balances out in the end.

How to Manage Your Nerves

Be the Duck
Even if a duck is paddling for his life, on the surface he still looks smooth, calm, collected, and in control. No matter what happens to you, just stay calm, and be the duck.

Reducing Nervousness
It's absolutely natural to be nervous in an interview, but it's how you handle the stress that will be the measure of your success. Here are two things you can do to get those butterflies under control.

1. Slow down your speech, and deepen your voice a tiny bit. When you're nervous, your voice tends to become higher and faster, so you end up falling over your words. If you slow your speech down and make your voice just a tad deeper, however, you'll be able to think more clearly and will feel more in control.
2. Be "other-oriented." It's tough to think about yourself and someone else at the same time, so if you focus on the person you're talking to, it shuts down your own self-focus, and you end up being less nervous.

Case in point: A candidate had just completed the first on-site interview. She got rave reviews all around, but the interviewers said she appeared nervous and had giggled too much. For the next round of interviews, I counseled her to slow down her speech, deepen her voice a tiny bit, and be other-oriented. She needed to be the duck. It worked like a charm and she was a lot less nervous, nailed the second interview, and got the job.

These two tricks might not calm your nerves to the same level as reading the Sunday comics and sipping a latte, but they will bring your heart rate down and help you feel more at ease.

Answering the Number-One Scariest Question
"Sooooo...what's your greatest weakness?" This is the question that strikes fear into every candidate's heart. How do you handle it? What's the best approach? What exactly should you say?

Simply put, your greatest weakness is actually your greatest strength taken to the extreme. And if you add a boundary (usually a time frame) to that weakness, you can even minimize the impact of that weakness.

For example, if your greatest strength is thinking strategically, then your greatest weakness is focusing *only* on strategy and forgetting to consider the tactical requirements needed to make the strategy work. Your interview answer might be, "I'm very strategic, but sometimes I can get too focused on the big picture, so I constantly rein back in and go to the tactical side to make sure the strategy makes sense."

If your greatest strength is your organizational ability, then your greatest weakness is imposing your organizational standards on others. Your interview answer might be, "I'm extremely organized, and although my kitchen pantry is color coded with a first-in-last-out inventory system, I don't impose my standards on my colleagues" Here, the boundary around the weakness is location (home versus work).

If your greatest strength is the ability to analyze massive amounts of data and see patterns, then your greatest weakness might be to overlook the personal or human factor and rely only on the data. Your interview answer might be, "I can become overly focused on the data, so I make myself stand back and look at the big picture on a daily basis to make sure I've not taken the data out of context."

By attaching a boundary it shows you're mature and self-aware enough to know your own faults, while also self-disciplined enough to do something to compensate.

> **Stories from the Trenches...**
>
> A job seeker emailed a note about his résumé: "I have a really poo work history."

How to Begin the Search

Structure Your Workday
Put in place a daily schedule for Monday to Friday.
- Get up at the same time every morning. Don't sleep late, or you'll find yourself getting up later every day.
- Take a shower, brush your hair, use deodorant, clean your teeth, and put on clean go-to-work clothes.
- Work on your search for at least five hours per day.
- Get some regular exercise...even if it's just a walk around the block.
- Drink plenty of water. You'll feel better if you're properly hydrated.
- Do some work around the house. If your old job was such that you weren't at home to help with children or chores, then it's important to pitch in now. A lot.
- Engage with family and friends, and enjoy time with them. You'll be back at work soon enough.
- Spend a little time each week volunteering.

Daily Log Sheet
Here's a handy checklist to keep track of your daily progress. You just record your start and end times, how much time you took for lunch, and what you accomplished. Each day, your goal is to earn at least twenty-five points. In this example, on Monday, Bob sent out five résumés, so that equals twenty-five points, and he hit his goal for the day. On Tuesday, he sent out three résumés and four follow-up emails; talked with three industry colleagues; and had a phone interview, earning forty-four points! A bonanza day!

Every day your goal is to get a job offer *or* an interview *or* twenty-five points. If you use this checklist faithfully, it'll help keep you on track, and at the end of each week, you'll be able to see the progress you've achieved. There's a photocopy-worthy version of this checklist on page 117.

Bob's Job Search	Monday	Tuesday	Wednesday	Thursday	Friday
Start time	9:00	9:00	9:15	9:00	9:00
Lunch	11 to 1	11 to 12	12 to 1	11 to 12	n/a
End time	4:00	3:30	4:00	3:30	1:00
Total time searching	5 hours	5 ½ hours	5 ¾ hours	5 ½ hours	4 hours
Resume submissions (5 points each)	͵卌	///	͵卌	͵卌	//
Follow-up on existing submissions (1 point each)	-0-	////	/	//	͵卌
Talk to anyone about the search (5 points each)	-0-	///	/	///	-0-
Phone interview (10 points each)	-0-	/	-0-	/	-0-
In-person interview (20 points each)	-0-	-0-	-0-	-0-	-0-
Volunteering (10 points each)	-0-	-0-	-0-	-0-	/
Total points — Goal is 25 points per day	25 points	44 points	31 points	52 points	25 points

How to Begin the Search

Aim to Submit Five Résumés per Day
Let's propose that it takes, say, fifty résumé submissions to get a job offer. If you send out two résumés a week, it'll take you twenty-five weeks to land an offer. If you send out five résumés a day, you'll achieve fifty submissions in two weeks. Since most interview processes typically take longer than two weeks, you likely won't get an offer at exactly the two-week mark, but you will increase your chances of getting, say, two offers in a month, or three offers in six weeks. Whatever the number of résumé submissions it ends up taking, it's just a case of simple statistics. If you send out enough résumés, you'll increase your visibility in the job market.

Sending out five résumés per day is hard work, but if you make it the basic building block of your "work" day, it'll keep you focused and feeling much more in control of your world. If you get to 5 p.m. on a Friday with no interviews or job offers to show for the week, you can still head into the weekend knowing you've sent out twenty-five résumés. And that is no small accomplishment!

Feedback from Someone Who Held to the Goal
Here's an email from someone who implemented the five-résumés-per-day goal.

> Jane,
> I wanted to give you a quick update: Following your sage advice to the best of my abilities, I have been pounding the digital sidewalk for the last 2 weeks. You suggested 5 quality applications a day, religiously, and with consistency. WOW! This is hard work! Filtering through the jobs I don't want, the ones that don't meet my income needs, and the ones that I think are good, then turn out to be clunkers. Can you imagine me in a pair of rubber boots running around the barn yard demonstrating products for milk extraction in a dairy? Apparently the manufacturer of said products couldn't either! I got the "while your credentials are impressive…." letter. We both dodged a bullet on that one!
>
> Anyway, here is the good part: This past Friday, I received calls from two major national manufacturers wanting to discuss my skills and resume. I spoke with HR at Company One for ten minutes and was told I would be passed on to the National Sales Manager for further consideration. Company Two emailed that they had chosen me to do a recorded Skype interview that same day and they would later review as a panel. I had never done one of those, but it was kind of fun. Today, Company One's National Sales Manager and I spoke for around 20 minutes. She then invited me to Tennessee for a panel interview with others on the Management team. Then, this afternoon someone from Company 3 called me and we spoke for 45 minutes. I don't know what will happen there, but I figure 45 minutes is probably a good sign for an initial screening.
>
> Enough bragging. Thank you, thank you, thank you! I appreciate your support, advice and help in formatting my resume. Regardless if any of these 3 bear fruit, I am still forging ahead trying to find the strong 5.

Finding five companies per day is a hard slog, but it pays dividends in the end.

Success, in large part, can be measured by what you do when things go wrong.

> **Stories from the Trenches…**
>
> Comment from a candidate: "Well, if you're flying by the seat of your pants, at least you're airborne."

How to Begin the Search

Indecision Isn't an Excuse for Inactivity
A sales rep had lost his job, so I checked in with him a month later to see how he was doing. He admitted he'd not done much with his search; his daughter had gotten married right after he lost his job, so there had been a lot of things to do with the run-up to the wedding. He said he and his wife had been thinking about relocating to a city a few hours away from their home, but again, he'd not done much in the way of investigation.

As his self-appointed guidance counselor, I told him he needed to be spending five hours a day on his job search...two hours on his current city and three hours on his desired location, plus an additional three hours a day getting their house ready to sell.

My reasoning was that if he'd had a phone interview with a company in the new location, the recruiter or hiring manager could ask, "How committed are you to moving?" If the candidate had already been spending three hours a day (or at least some decent amount of time) readying his house for sale, he'd be able to rattle off a list of things he'd done to prepare, which would be a clear indication that he was, indeed, serious about relocation.

I suggested he was using the possibility of a relocation as an excuse to do nothing with his job search in either location. He emailed me a few weeks later and said, "Thank you for the much-needed kick in the pants."

The Value of Volunteering
Unemployment can bring moments/hours/days/weeks where you feel adrift with no definition and no purpose. Self-confidence can plummet like a roller coaster at full tilt, and it's exhausting clawing your way back. To help you stay grounded, try to spend a few hours each week volunteering in a soup kitchen or homeless shelter. It can be anywhere, really...just so long as you enjoy the work and are lending a hand.

Case in point: When I started Northstar Recruiting, the nation was in the throes of the dot.com crash. My timing for starting a business could not have been worse, and I had countless gut-wrenching hours/days/weeks wondering what I was playing at. To balance out this exercise in futility, I volunteered a couple of times a week at a local homeless shelter, and it helped put life in perspective. When I'd had a bad day at the office, serving soup at the shelter kept me grateful. When I'd had a good day at the office, serving that soup kept me humble.

Guard Your Time
When you're unemployed, family, friends, or neighbors might think you're home binge-watching Netflix and have lots of free time to be at their beck and call, so be protective of your job-search time.

It's genuine targeted activity, not busyness, that will give you forward motion toward your goals.

Stories from the Trenches...

Seen on LinkedIn: "My goal is to become a Life Insurance Sales Consultant, a Registered Nurse, a Stock Market Trading Firm, and a US Ambassador, all at the same time."

How to Begin the Search

It Could Take a While, so Conserve Cash
Regardless of whether the economy is booming or tanking, you'll be better equipped financially and emotionally if you anticipate your search taking at least six months. Conserving cash is imperative, so take a hard look at your household expenses, and cut out as many extras as possible. If you land a job sooner than expected, you'll have cash to spare. If your search stretches out longer than expected, you'll thank yourself for having reduced the cash outflow.

Money Management
Know what your household budget is, and clean up your credit history.

I had a candidate who was perfect for a role, but the credit check showed he'd declared bankruptcy, which wasn't an issue at all, but he still had numerous outstanding debts, which were listed as "Refusal to pay." This was a poor reflection on his character, so he was out of the running for the job. Not all companies check credit history, but it's good to have checked your history, just in case.

For money management guidance, Dave Ramsey's Financial Peace University is a super resource.

Unearth Your Old W-2s
You're not required to divulge your earnings, but you should at least know what you've made over the last few years so you'll know how much you need to stay on par. To verify, dig up the last few years' W-2s and double-check.

Do What It Takes to Survive
Here's a note from a sales executive who lost his job in late 2014.

> I took a job in the lumber yard at Home Depot. Not something I wanted to do long-term, but it's a good company. Even as a part-time employee, there were benefits…medical and 401K. I needed to get out of the house and bring in some gas money. Working with people who make $9.50 per hour for 22.5 hours a week (most have two jobs, some have three jobs) you gain a perspective as to what people are going through. Salt of the earth people who work hard.

This executive landed a director's role in July 2015, but just the mere fact that he stepped out of his comfort zone and became an hourly wage earner at a home improvement store spoke volumes about his work ethic and character.

He was proud of his career, but not at all prideful. He was a rock star in my book!

Your job is to find a job, and consistent searching will be the key to success. Establish your process and hold to it…even when you don't want to.

Stories from the Trenches…

A conversation with a new candidate:
Me: "How are your writing skills?"
Candidate: "They're very strong! I started out as an English major."
Me: "Great! What's your opinion of the Oxford comma?"
Candidate (after a long pause, he gave this very witty response): "Weeeeellll…I guess my writing skills aren't that great."

How to Begin the Search

Clean Up Your Social Media Pages
It's vital that you sanitize all your social media accounts and delete anything that might be interpreted as risky or risqué. It's impossible to predict how a picture might be perceived, so it's best to err on the side of caution.

You absolutely can adopt the philosophy of "Accept me as I am, or I just don't wanna know ya." But that's not a mature attitude, and you won't get far with it. Just be a grown-up, and clean up your accounts.

Attention, students! Even though you might not be job hunting now, you will be one day, and once an image is out there, you cannot un-ring that bell. Be smart about what you post.

The Interviewing Paradox
If you have a stable work history, you likely haven't spent much time job hunting and interviewing, so you end up repeating the same mistakes every time you do conduct a search.

If you have job-hopped, you're likely more at ease with the search process, but you're a flight risk because you don't stay with a company long term.

So where's the balance? That is an age-old question. If you have changed companies too often, then it might be time to settle down. If you're not experienced with interviewing, then preparation and practice will help you feel more comfortable.

Get Organized and Stay Organized
Keep track of where your resumes goes, including the following:
- The job boards where you post your résumé.
- The job opportunities for which you apply.
- The recruiters to whom you send your résumé and the companies to which they send your résumé.
- All those colleagues and friends to whom you send your résumé.

Should You Use the Job Boards?
Yes, absolutely! Hiring managers, HR professionals, and third-party recruiters are mining job boards constantly, so utilize these sites to the fullest. You might get a ton of inquiries asking if you want to sell insurance, but ignore them (unless, of course, selling insurance is what you want to do), and just view the job boards as an exercise in panning for gold.

Slips of the tongue are like rivets holding a ship's hull together. If too many go flying, you're sunk.

Stories from the Trenches...

A candidate pointed out that, "...people who insist they are logical thinkers are by no means implying they are *reasonable* thinkers. Rather, they are explaining that the only logic by which they can exist is their own. Reasonable or not, they leave no room for the priorities and opinions of others. Beware the logical ones, for they are not necessarily reasonable."

How to Begin the Search

Don't Marry the Job
Even if a job description clearly has your name written all over it and is 100 percent perfect for you, *do not marry it!* So many times, a candidate has seen a job description and fallen in love, then stopped searching because the perfect job clearly has arrived. Maybe the interviews were awesome, and an offer is "on the way." But then, silence. Calls and emails to the company go unanswered, and the candidate is left stranded at the altar with no ring, no "I do," and no other opportunities in the pipeline as a backup.

It is totally okay to fall in love with a job opportunity, but *keep searching* while it plays out. Only stop looking when you have a signed offer in hand, your background check is complete, and your start date is scheduled.

Preconceived Notions
When you've had a bad experience in a particular type of work environment, say in a start-up company, there may be a tendency to shy away from similar roles for fear they'll turn out to be just as painful. But don't kick these opportunities to the curb too fast.

Any bad experience can help you develop a more fine-tuned antenna and a whole new set of questions you can use to gain a clearer understanding of an environment. If the role is of interest to you, go ahead and interview for it. Just make sure to ask some pointed questions that'll let you uncover whether it would be history repeating itself, or if it's really something quite different.

Additional Education Isn't Necessarily the Answer
Don't jump to the conclusion that you need additional certifications or coursework to enhance your skills. Before starting anything, look on LinkedIn to see what education or training the majority of people have in the role. Is that additional certification commonplace? Or is the additional education maybe just a way for you to postpone having to spend time conducting the search?

If the additional education truly would give you more options, then dig deeper into the costs and the scheduling feasibility. If it won't help you down the road, then scratch it off your list.

Be Prepared to Kiss a Lot of Frogs
A lot of conversations won't lead anywhere, but be polite and considerate through all, because you just never know what'll surface down the road. If you're not interested in continuing a conversation, exit *respectfully.*

You Have to Lose Count
If you're actively conducting a search and you can name every company to which you've applied, then you haven't applied to enough places. You basically have to be so prolific in your résumé submissions that it's impossible to recount them all.

You are an average of the top five people with whom you spend your time. Are you impressed by them or shamed by them?

> **Stories from the Trenches...**
>
> After a very long interview process, I asked a newly placed candidate how he was handling not having to talk to me every day. He said, "It's a white knuckle ride, but I'm hanging in there and have a twelve-step program."

Handling the Compensation Question

The $$ Question
Most people hate the compensation question, so let's put that fish on the table and tackle it right now.

Some states prohibit the question "What are you earning?" But you still can be asked what compensation you are *requiring*.

It would be foolish for a recruiter to proceed too far into any conversation without first making sure you're in the price range, so when someone does pose the salary question, go ahead and divulge both what you're earning and what you're looking for. If it's not a match, you've just saved time and effort that can be better spent elsewhere.

The Likely Conversation
Here's a sample conversation about salary.

Me: What was your salary at ABC Company? (Assuming the candidate lives where this question is permitted.)
Candidate: My salary was $100K, and last year I earned a total of $120K with bonus.
Me: What salary and on-target earnings are you looking for in your next role?

Nice potential responses:
    . . . I'd consider a fair and equitable offer.
    . . . I'd like to stay close to that base and total earnings.
    . . . I believe I'm underpaid here, so I am looking for something of an increase.
    . . . I'm due for a raise in two months, so I'd like to get a bump up in salary to stay on par with where I'll be.
    . . . I'd prefer not to go backward in earnings.
    . . . I've lived below my means, so I'm flexible and can take a cut if it's the right role.
    . . . Since this will be my first job out of college, I'm open to the going market rate.
    . . . Wuuuunnnn miiiillion dollars and a car. . .but I'm totally flexible on the color. (A little humor can go a long way if you time it right.)

Each of these responses (except for that last one) is direct and invites further conversation.

Whatever you do decide to say, practice it out loud a few dozen times *before* the interview. Repeat it until it becomes second nature and you barely even have to think about it. Doing this will help ensure you come across as polished, genuine, and at ease.

If a salary range is too low for you, do not in any way be sarcastic. Don't say, "Your loss!" If you do mouth off, you won't ever get a call back, even if the salary range increases or when a better-paying gig surfaces. Then that would just be *your* loss.

Don't Bring Up Pay
Never, never, never in any shape or form ask, "How much does the job pay?" Let the interviewer bring up the topic of salary—then reply as you've practiced, and then ask if you're within the range.

> Aim for that fine line between not appearing to be greedy while also not leaving any money on the table. Write out what you want to say and practice it out loud. Record yourself to see how you're truly coming across.

Stories from the Trenches...

Seen on a LinkedIn profile: "The only thing that overcomes hard luck is hard work."

Voicemail

Your Phone Is Your Lifeline
Take time to make sure that it is possible for a caller to leave you a message. Check for messages often, and empty out the box regularly. If your voice mail is full, you will never know what you missed.

If you list a telephone number that's likely to be answered by someone else, it's crucial the person answering your calls understands that politeness is the order of the day for every single call.

Making an impression starts from the point of first contact, and that includes the phone call.

Your Outgoing Voice Mail Message
One memorable voice message was "You've reached my voice mail...bummer."

Another was "You've reached the voice mail for Bob; he can't take your call, but leave your message, and if you're lucky, he'll call you back." Then there's the perennial favorite, "Hello...hello...hahahaha...I'm not here."

Really? Who wants to hire a smart-mouth?

For an Appropriate Outgoing Message, Do This:
- Write out your message, and practice it out loud before recording it. Be concise, professional, and clear.
- Record your message yourself.

Don't Do This:
- Don't start your voicemail message with, "Hey, hey, hey!"
- Don't get someone else to record your message for you, especially your children. It's not nearly as cute as you think it is. Don't have your assistant leave your outgoing message...that just makes you appear arrogant.
- Don't ad lib, and don't try to be funny.
- Don't have any noise in the background...no TV, radio, running water, dishwashing, cooking, beeping microwaves, squealing brakes, crying/screaming children, crying/screaming passengers, or drive-through attendant taking your bagel/coffee/lunch order.
- Don't use the phrase "at my earliest convenience." Your intent might be to let the caller know you'll reply as soon as possible, but the phrase "at my earliest convenience" means you'll call when it's convenient for you. But it's not about you...it's all about the caller.

Appropriate Outgoing Messages
Here are some sample scripts for your outgoing message.

> This is_____. I'm so sorry I missed your call, and if you'll leave me your name and number, I'll get back in touch with you as soon as I can. Thank you for calling.

> You've reached the voicemail for_____; please leave your name and number, and I'll return your call as soon as possible.

> This is_____. Thank you for your call, and I'm so sorry to have missed you. Please leave your name and number, and I'll reply back as soon as possible.

> **Stories from the Trenches...**
>
> A candidate's comment: "Escape velocity can be mental, emotional, or geographic."

Basic Phone Etiquette

When You Answer the Phone
If your phone rings and you don't recognize the caller, consider letting the call go to voice mail. It's far better to call someone back when you're in a quiet place surrounded by your notes than to get caught flat-footed and have to struggle through a conversation.

I've had countless conversations resembling this exchange:

Me: Hi, this is Jane Snipes with Northstar, and I'm returning your call.
Person I'm calling: Uh, who are you with?
Me: This is Jane at Northstar—you left me a message an hour ago regarding your job search, and I'm just calling you back.
Person I'm calling: Uhhhhh. . . I can't talk right now. I'm. . .
  . . . in a very important meeting. *(If you're in an important meeting, why are you answering the phone?)*
  . . . I'm in the bathroom. *(Are you kidding me?)*
  . . . I'm on a conference call. *(Did you remember to hit "mute" before you answered my call? Just sayin'!)*

If you can't talk freely, then let the call go to voice mail. It's what voice mail is for.

Don't Have a Personal Screener
Never, ever allow anyone to screen your calls. It rarely ends well.

Case in point: A job seeker had listed his résumé on Monster, so I called to introduce myself and run past him an opportunity that I thought might be a good match. His wife answered the phone and proceeded to grill me on the opportunity. She said, "He's going through me for his job search, so if you can't tell me the company name, then he won't be interested." Ohhhhhkaaayyyyyy, then.

While You're on the Phone
We've all become a bit numb to common courtesy and tend to think it's okay to take calls anywhere. But you should be vigilant at all times and be aware of your surroundings.

Incoming Calls
If you're in the middle of a phone conversation and you have an incoming call...don't click over. Let the incoming call go to voice mail, then ring back when you're clear of the first call. If you feel you have to catch that incoming call, then click over and say something like, "I'm not where I can talk at the moment, but I didn't want you to bounce to voice mail. May I call you back in a few minutes?"

Do not ask the caller to ring you back! The onus is on you to get their contact information and for *you* to call *them* back.

Make sure you hang up the phone properly. And if you're not going to answer an incoming call, make sure you hit "decline" instead of "answer."

> **Stories from the Trenches...**
>
> During a phone interview, the candidate yelled at someone: "Get your ass back in this car." Yikes!

Basic Phone Etiquette

What Not to Do while Talking on the Phone
- Do not talk to your dog.
- Do not open a squeaky door. Go get some WD-40, and fix it before the call.
- Do not rock in your chair if it squeaks. Where's that WD-40? You'd be surprised how sounds are transmitted through the phone, and a simple chair squeak on your end might sound like a bad case of gas on the other end of the line.
- Do not have just stepped out of the shower...and then announce that fact to the caller.
- Do not flush the toilet.
- Do not wash your hands or the dishes.
- Do not heat coffee/food/anything in the microwave.
- Do not yell at your children. It doesn't matter who's doing what to whom. Try hand signals instead.
- Do not smoke...we can hear you exhale.
- Don't tell the caller what you're doing. One person answered his phone while standing on a ladder reworking some electrical wiring. Just stop already. You don't have to answer your phone every time it rings.
- Do not curse or use any expletives in any way, shape, or form.

Have full 360-degree awareness of your surroundings
Avoid these situations:
- Barking dogs
- The store checkout line
- The drive-through
- The bathroom (I know, I know...it's a reoccurring theme here.)
- A loud sporting event or a busy mall
- The gate at the airport while you're waiting to board
- Your airplane seat
- Being in bed...especially if it's after 8 o'clock in the morning. If you're in bed sick, that's a different story, but if you're fine and just sleeping in, don't answer your phone! If you do, the caller will know you're lying down. Oh, and don't ever say, "I'm just now waking up" or "I'm still in my jammies."
- Do not attempt to multitask while on the phone. If you make a mistake, you just can't un-ring that bell.

Unavoidable Interruptions
If you do have a situation that's unavoidable, just apologize for the interruption, and move back to the conversation as quickly as possible. If the interruption is really too distracting, ask if you can call the interviewer back in just a minute. You don't need to give a detailed description of the interruption—just take care of it, then get back to the conversation.

The best defense is a good offense, so make sure you eliminate distractions prior to the call. Whatever happens, if you have grace under fire, it can earn you points.

When Leaving Your Information
Don't say, "Hi, it's me!" You should speak your full name and phone number at a reasonable pace. If you blister through at warp speed, the receiver will have to replay your message over and over to figure out what you said. Just give the information at a pace that's understandable, and make sure to repeat your phone number.

> **Stories from the Trenches...**
>
> A job title seen on LinkedIn: "Freelance witness."

LinkedIn

It's a Super Tool
LinkedIn truly is a remarkable tool and one you should fully use to your advantage. Having a profile is totally normal—in fact, not having one these days might be considered shortsighted, particularly for sales and marketing professionals.

What if Your Boss Sees Your LinkedIn Profile?
Your LinkedIn profile is the electronic version of your business card and a means of communication, so updating your profile doesn't necessarily mean you're conducting a job search. If you *do* want to stay below the radar, though, you can go to your privacy settings and select the option that your network *will not* be notified when you make changes to your profile.

You can also make changes slowly over a few weeks or months in order to help keep you invisible.

Or you can just list what your company does and wordsmith it to include key words that are pertinent to your own role.

Confidential Profile over Full Disclosure
The whole point of LinkedIn is expansion of your professional network, so if you don't want to show your name, then why sign up in the first place?

If you are actively conducting a search, a fully disclosed profile helps increase your visibility, and I recommend choosing settings that allow anyone to send you an invite to connect or an InMail.

Listing Your Contact Information
If you're actively job searching, make it easy for recruiters to reach you by listing your contact information in the Summary section of your profile. To get to the Summary, go to "Me", click on "View Profile," then click on the little edit pencil in the right hand corner of the "About" section.

It All Needs to Match
When you submit your résumé to a company, the recruiter will likely compare the dates on your résumé to those on your LinkedIn profile. If the dates don't match up, it can make you look careless, so double-check that everything's consistent. It's *your* profile and *your* responsibility to ensure accuracy.

Double-Check Those End Dates
Be especially diligent in adding end dates to those roles you've already left. If you list a previous role as Current, it looks like you're double-dipping. If you have several entries that show Current when you've already left all of them, then you just look sloppy.

If you are actually working multiple jobs simultaneously, then having Current is totally accurate and no problem at all.

> **Don't try and trick someone by reversing your name in your LinkedIn profile. If your name is, say, Robert Smith, don't list yourself as "Smith Robert."**

Stories from the Trenches…

Reply on LinkedIn: "Sounds like my current job…am I being replaced? LOL!"

LinkedIn

How Much Information to List?
I recommend listing all your job titles and, if possible, attaching the company's logo to each employment entry. Make sure you spell your company's name correctly.

In order to maximize the number of key word hits you get, cut and paste all your experience and accomplishment details from your résumé into your LinkedIn profile.

Key Word Count
Key words are crucial on your LinkedIn profile. When a recruiter conducts a search, the resulting list will have the profile with the greatest number of key word hits at the top—and that profile with the least number of key word hits at the bottom. Everyone else is ranked accordingly in between.

Not every LinkedIn member lists all their information on their profile, so any search list that's generated doesn't actually reflect reality. It's just mirroring the number of key word matches available at that moment in time. Since there's no guarantee a recruiter will look at every single profile on the search list, you need to be as close to the top of the list as possible in order to increase your chances of having your profile reviewed. To get closer to the top of the list, you just need more key words in your profile. To increase your key words, you just have to put all the employment details from your résumé into your LinkedIn profile. If you've already done the updates to your résumé, it's simply a matter of cutting and pasting the information into your LinkedIn profile, and voila—you've increased your visibility!

InMails and Invites to Connect
If you're job hunting, you should set your LinkedIn profile so that anyone can send you an InMail or invite to connect. You're not obligated to accept an invite or InMail, but it will be odd if you're open to opportunities but don't want to hear from anyone. Just as with the job boards, you will have to put up with some spam, but buried in all that noise might be a golden opportunity.

Do use your personal email address for your LinkedIn profile. If you use a work address and you've left the company, then you won't receive notifications when a new InMail or invite shows up.

Multiple LinkedIn Profiles
Check to see if you have multiple profiles on LinkeIn and get rid of any duplicates. The LinkedIn Help Center has details on how to delete them.

Listing Your LinkedIn Profile Link on Your Résumé
It's totally okay to include a link to your profile on your résumé. Just put it alongside your email address, and make sure it's the short format that includes your name, not the long form that's just a string of random characters.

> *If you use your work email address for LinkedIn, don't get mad when InMails from recruiters show up in your work inbox.*

Stories from the Trenches...

One individual listed that he was responsible for "...collaboration and consummation."

LinkedIn

Your Profile Picture

If a recruiter is going through a list of profiles and sees an unprofessional picture, they might skip over that profile completely. To be clear, if you're not looking for a job, then post whatever picture you want. If you *are* looking for a job, however, then choose your picture wisely. This is my rule of no Bs. No...

- baseball caps, especially worn backward,
- beer,
- bars—neither the traditional walk-in type nor the swim-up type,
- boats nor bikes,
- body parts that belong to other people (shoulder, chin, hair, ear, hand, elbow...the list goes on),
- bare belly (your own or anyone else's),
- back of your head,
- Bambi or any other animal (domesticated or not),
- bathroom accessories of any sort (this includes towel rods, mirrors, showers, bathtubs, and commodes),
- beds and any bed accoutrements,
- bedroom eyes gazing into the camera,
- bedhead hair to any degree,
- boob tubes or off-the-shoulder tops (FYI, you just look naked).

One memorable profile picture was of a young man wearing a ripped sleeveless T-shirt and a backward baseball cap. He was sitting on a boat in the middle of a lake, holding a beer, and looking away from the camera. He had so many Bs I lost count. It's been ten years, but I still remember that picture: It's the benchmark of what *not* to do.

The ideal profile picture has...
- A plain background.
- Good lighting so your face can be seen.
- An in-focus picture.
- You fully dressed in formal business or high-end business casual attire.
- You looking directly at the camera.
- A nice smile.
- A head-and-shoulders picture.

I recommend you avoid...
- Having any of the above Bs in your picture.
- Having your face in the shade such that you're indecipherable.
- Loosening your tie like you're at the end of a long day.
- Taking a picture of a picture—it'll just be too grainy.
- Frowning, scowling, or attempting to look studious. It just comes across weird.
- Showing your midriff, cleavage, six-pack abs, or any other body part traditionally covered by clothing.
- Having a drink in your hand or anywhere near you.
- Anything connected to the interior of a car or aircraft.
- Taking a picture of yourself in front of a mirror such that the phone is also in the picture.
- Having anyone else in the picture—it'll be unclear who's who.
- Pretending to talk on the phone.
- Holding a firearm.
- Anything related to a wedding.
- The picture of you at a lectern giving a presentation.
- The picture of you holding a microphone...even if it was the best karaoke song ever!
- Squinting. It doesn't make you look thoughtful; it makes you look constipated or flatulent.

LinkedIn

A Few Examples of Profile Pictures

Your LinkedIn picture shouldn't look too different from how you look now. You don't want to show up for a video or in-person interview and have the interviewer's first response be one of surprise because you don't look like your picture.

> Never use a picture with the word "Proof" stamped across the front; to do so is stealing from the photographer. Your picture is a direct reflection of your professionalism and judgement, so pick wisely. It's better to use no picture than the wrong picture.

Stories from the Trenches...

How people have been described by their manager:
"Skilled but odd. May keep pet insects at home."
"A refugee from a Grateful Dead concert...but skilled."
"Young, eager, not a great communicator, but could moonlight as an underwear model."
"Skilled and way into video games. Might be years since his last date but he really knows his stuff."
"Actually normal...so I'm not sure how good he is."

Where to Find Job Opportunities

Where to Look
Go online and look up "list of major job boards." The most well-known boards right now are LinkedIn, Monster, CareerBuilder, Glassdoor, Dice, and Indeed, but there are a plethora of others out there, so scope out as many as you can. Also look at these options:

- Your university alumni placement and networking services
- Job fairs
- Third-party recruiters
- Temporary services
- Your own network

Each conversation is a chance to maximize your visibility and to fine-tune your interviewing skills, so investigate every lead as far as you can take it.

How to Find Third-Party Recruiters
To start building a list of recruiters, go through these steps:

- Visit Management Recruiters International (MRI) at www.mrinetwork.com and follow the prompts to search for jobs and recruiters.
  1. Use key words to find recruiters in your industry or job function.
     FYI: Geographic location of the recruiter doesn't matter at all. If the recruiter's specialty matches the job and industry you seek, then the recruiter could be working remotely from a beach hut in Fiji and still conduct business.

  2. Make a list of all the MRI recruiting offices that match your industry or function, then reach out to each.
     FYI: Almost all the MRI offices are individually owned, so they're very insular and, for all intents and purposes, compete with each other. Since they are all separate, contact each office where there is a recruiter matching your specialty. If an office has multiple recruiters matching your specialty, contact just one recruiter per office.

- For a broader general search, look online for "executive recruiters," and then narrow down to your chosen industry or function, and follow the same process for these independent recruiters as you did for the MRI recruiters.

- For each job posting you come across, check to see if it's a third-party recruiter who's conducting the search. If it is, email the recruiter and introduce yourself, as there may be other job opportunities that might be a match for you. The recruiter might also be able to refer you to someone else who can help you.

Company Size
If you don't want to be bound by the strict confines of a job description, you might be happier in a small to midsize company. Large companies will have more hierarchy and bureaucracy, so you might have a more defined boundary surrounding your job duties.

If you're chewing gum or food, then chew with your mouth closed. It doesn't matter how good-looking or intelligent you are; if you chew with your mouth open, you'll look dumb as a stump.

How to Work with Third-Party Recruiters

Assume They're Good Guys
Most third-party recruiters work on 100 percent commission, so the bad ones eventually starve and go find something else to do. Of those who are left, a few will be fantastic, and the rest will be average. If you're actively conducting a search, then work with anyone and everyone, since even the not-so-good recruiters have great job opportunities. If you're just passively looking, you can be more choosy.

In any situation, if a recruiter doesn't treat you properly, just vote with your feet and walk away.

You Get to Choose
You're in charge of your own job search, so in your first conversation with a third-party recruiter, let them know your résumé should not be submitted to any company without first checking with you.

The Proverbial Alligator-and-Bridge Situation
In a healthy economy with low unemployment, people get deluged with inquiries from recruiters, so it's tempting to either ignore recruiters' emails or reply back with a terse "Get lost!" In a down economy, though, recruiters can become your best friend—so, to help ensure a recruiter will be there to help you when you need it, always be polite and try to make a point of responding to inquires…even if the message is, "Not right now, but thanks so much anyway!" If you're short, terse, curt, or rude in any way, the recruiter will likely make a note of it and will be less likely to work with you down the road.

Keep Copious Notes
It's your responsibility to make sure your résumé isn't presented to a company by multiple recruiters, so you must keep careful track of where your résumé goes. If your résumé is submitted by multiple recruiters, it might make you look like you're not in control of your own search.

The Difference between Being Judgmental and Having Good Judgment
Third-party recruiters have the shelf life of a fruit fly and are only as good as the last interview they arranged. If they trip up, there's a line of other sharks waiting to step in and capture their client's attention.

While it's not the recruiter's place to judge you or your decisions, it is their responsibility to judge whether you'll be a good match for their client, so don't take it personally if you don't get moved forward in the process. Most searches are commission-based, so it's not in a recruiter's best interests to withhold a solid candidate. Whatever happens, just be professional. If you argue back, it'll only reduce your chances of being considered for a future vacancy.

> Don't tell a recruiter all the companies you're interviewing with, as they might back-door you and try to get in on the search in order to present their own candidates. And don't let any recruiter talk you into working with them exclusively. Just play the field, and network as much as you can.

Stories from the Trenches…

The best reference comment I ever heard: "You can replace him, but you'll never replace his performance."

How to Work With Third-Party Recruiters

How Not to Work with Third-Party Recruiters

For some comic relief, here's an email exchange from 2014. A candidate I'd placed many years prior was trying to help someone out with their job search and had made the introduction to me. I've changed the names to protect the innocent.

Bob is the person who was trying to be helpful.

Sam is the person who lived in Orange County, California, whom Bob was trying to help.

In the early email exchange, I explained to Sam that although I didn't have any job opportunities open in Orange County at that time, I'd welcome the chance to talk in case anything came open. Here's the follow-up email exchange as Sam expressed his displeasure at making my acquaintance.

Sam's email to me telling me to get lost: "I have a few very qualified recruiters and networkers that are very interested in placing me or helping me. Thank you for your interest but I prefer to work with local recruiters and networkers."

Sam's email to Bob and me expressing his annoyance at being introduced to me: "I am not sure why, but you have forwarded my credentials to an out of state recruiter—Jane Snipes working out of Florence, South Carolina! She does not have any local connections here in Orange County and I don't feel she will be the best to represent my skills and expertise to any Orange County Entity.
I am NOT interested to relocate out of Orange County, CA!
Please feel free to forward my résumé to local Orange County recruiters only."

Bob's email to Sam explaining why he made the initial introduction: "Sam, Jane works with companies all over the world in the industry. She has a long client list, and you never know."

Sam's email to Bob and me: "Even though you, Jane, may have some local connections, it's not the same in my humble opinion, as local recruiters that focus here in Orange County.
Accordingly, I prefer to work with local recruiters EXCLUSIVELY."

My email to Bob: "Wow. He's a gem isn't he? Thanks for trying, though!"

Bob's email to me: "Yes, and glad we are seeing this now. Predict he will be searching for quite some time."

Sam was seriously qualified for a top role, but his interpersonal skills were poor at best. I doubt I'd have had a job opportunity open for him in his location, but his shortsightedness in not wanting to expand his network was just a symptom of his inability to play well with other kids in the sandbox. Who knows what opportunities he's missed because of it?

It's been six years since that email exchange, and I just looked up Sam on LinkedIn. It took him five months to land in a new role, and since May 2015, he's had three different jobs. As of early 2020, he is unemployed.

> **Don't look a gift horse in the mouth. You don't have to engage with third-party recruiters, but do be pleasant—you just never know what'll come of it.**

Stories from the Trenches…

A candidate felt he hadn't done well in a couple of interviews and begged me to please tell him why. I told him it might be because he sometimes comes across as knowing everything. He hung up.

How to Work With Third-Party Recruiters

If You Make a Mistake

If you misstep and just can't shake that feeling of remorse or regret, then write a brief apology—then it'll be off your plate and out of your head.

Case in point: I'd presented a sales candidate to a manager, and the manager wanted to schedule an interview, but the candidate wouldn't respond to my queries regarding his availability to talk. About two months later, the candidate called me to see what had happened to the job opportunity. I told him I'd tried to reach him but that he'd never replied. He said he'd been slammed and asked if he could be reconsidered, but I told him no. He also called me Sandy, which actually wasn't too bad at all, as I have been called a lot worse.

Here's his follow-up note a few days after our conversation.

> Hello Jane,
> I felt horrible after our call Thursday. Wanted to send you a quick note and apologize.
>
> I was working a couple of deals this last month that could make my year's quota. Everything else went on the back burner. It's a trait that has helped me at work, but it is no excuse for my actions with you.
>
> After our conversation, I realized how self involved I have been. Not responding back to you sooner was rude and disrespectful. I am sorry. Thank you again for presenting me with a great opportunity. Sorry I let you down.
>
> If there is ever anything I can help you with, then please do not hesitate to ask!

He made a mistake, but he took ownership of it and apologized, which gave us the opportunity to reset our relationship and put it back onto a fresh footing.

Decision Postponement

If you have an initial conversation with a recruiter, but you're on the fence about whether to pursue an opportunity or not, then give yourself a few days to think about it. If the opportunity keeps percolating to the forefront of your brain, then maybe it's worth at least an initial conversation. If, on the other hand, you totally forget about it, then it's a solid sign it's not the one for you. If you've promised the recruiter a follow-up, keep to your word, and send a note thanking them for their time while also gracefully bowing out.

> 💡 If you're not sure how to pronounce the company name, call their customer service number and ask. Then write it down phonetically so you'll have a reminder.

> **Stories from the Trenches...**
>
> The coolest resignation ever was when a candidate accepted an offer and went in to work to resign. Before he could talk to his boss, however, he was pulled into a meeting with seven other senior employees and told their jobs had been cut. He was awarded twenty-two weeks of severance pay and four weeks' notice of separation. In total, he got six months' pay; plus, he already had a new job lined up. Boom!

General Résumé Submissions

How to Reach Out
Check out the recruiting company's or hiring company's website, and look for instructions on how to apply for employment. Those instructions will undoubtedly say to email your résumé, and you should abide by those instructions to the letter. Even if you don't agree with the process, follow it anyway.

If you call the recruiter without first sending a résumé, the recruiter won't have any background information on you, so you'll catch them flat-footed. You'll likely get brushed off and asked to email your résumé, so just email your résumé first, then wait a day or so before following up. Don't call ten minutes after hitting Send and ask, "Did you get my résumé?"

The Best Introduction
The best introduction is a very brief email with your résumé attached in both Word and PDF. I received these notes via LinkedIn and really liked the approach because both were short, professionally friendly, and very respectful.

> Hi Jane, I am a Digital Transformation Solutions Sales Executive located in NC, and am looking for a new role. Please keep me in network & in mind as you seek Strategic Growth Leaders.

> Hello, Jane. In the past few months things here have changed dramatically, so much so that I may be looking for something new. Is it possible we could work together?

Salutations
Always include a greeting in your email note. If you don't, your email will look like spam and will be treated as such.

If you have the recipient's email address and their name is obvious, then address your email to the individual. If you only have part of the recipient's name, then search on LinkedIn for the person's full name.

If the recipient's name isn't obvious, then go with "Good morning!" or "Good afternoon!" whichever is applicable to the time of day you're hitting Send.

Don't send an email to *Dear Company,* and don't use the recipient's first and last name, because it sounds too canned. I've received emails addressed to *Dear Ms. Jane Snipes, Dear Sirs, Dear North Star, Dear Decision Maker,* and even *Hello {Name},* all of which demonstrated a certain degree of thoughtlessness on the part of the sender.

Oh, and never send your résumé out in an email blast to "all contacts." If you can't be bothered to take the time to send an individual email, why should anyone take the time to reply?

Do not email a link to your Google doc resume. It's not likely accessible and not easily uploaded to a database. Instead, send your résumé in both Word and PDF formats.

Stories from the Trenches...

This is a non-work related application story, but still chuckle-worthy. A friend was completing a DMV application and read the questions aloud to her twelve-year-old son. His responses:
Would you like to be an organ donor?: "Well...not today."
Race: "Human."
Sex: "Why do they want to know how many times you've had sex?"

General Résumé Submissions

The Tone to Take
With every single email, maintain a professional, friendly tone. If you don't like the answer you get, be polite anyway so you can position yourself for future discussions.

Send It Yourself
Never rely on your spouse/significant other/parent to submit your résumé for you. While it is absolutely okay for a professional colleague to forward on your résumé, it's not appropriate for you to have someone else send out all your general résumé submissions. It's your search, and you should be the one doing the work.

Addressing a Mismatch
If you know that your résumé isn't a match for a particular role but you'd like to be on the recruiter's radar screen, then make mention of the criteria mismatch in your email.

For example, if you're in the wrong location but are willing to relocate, then mention your openness to moving. If you don't have the required experience, then state that you would welcome the chance to be considered if the criteria relaxes, or if another role opens up.

If your résumé clearly doesn't match the criteria and you've *not* bridged that gap with an explanation, you'll come across as being unrealistic and will likely end up being completely sidelined.

How and When to Follow Up
It is a bit of a guessing game, but if you set up guidelines for yourself, it takes the emotion out of the equation and becomes easier to handle.

Once you've sent over a résumé, wait a day or two, and then send another email. The note might be something like this:

> Just wanted to follow up on my email from yesterday and make sure you received my résumé. I'd welcome the chance to be considered for the role of ___ and would be glad to talk via phone if you feel I'm a match.

If you don't hear back in a week, then either call and leave a message, or send a third email. Do not say anything that might be perceived as passive aggressive. Leaving a message of, "Well, I guess you don't think I'm qualified or worth your time!" will absolutely ensure you never get a call back. Regardless of what happens, maintain that professionally friendly and respectful tone.

Nothin' but Crickets
When I'm conducting a search for candidates, I make two attempts to reach someone. If there's no reply after my second attempt, I move on. If the person happens to surface down the road, that's great. If not, I've just saved myself time and energy focusing on something that wasn't going to work in the first place. I adhere to the don't-marry-it guideline too!

If you don't hear back after three attempts, then take the opportunity off your radar screen. You don't know what's happening behind the scenes, so even if your background is perfect for the role and the job was clearly written for you, just let it go. If a response does arrive later, don't be critical of the delay—just go with the flow and see where the conversation takes you.

> **Stories from the Trenches…**
>
> A candidate said: "Be willing to throw yourself on your sword. Practice by throwing yourself on a splinter."

You Got a Response!

What to Do When You Get a Reply
You're judged and evaluated from the point of first contact, so always be polite, genuinely interested, and completely engaged. Be cognizant of the natural ebb and flow of the conversation, and if the interviewer interrupts you, you should stop talking!

The more desperate you are to find a job, the greater the tendency to talk nonstop in an attempt to tell your whole story in one long run-on sentence. Don't do this. Maintain self-control and avoid verbal diarrhea at all costs. Let the interviewer drive the discussion, and if you're a match for the vacancy, you'll be moved forward in the process. If you're not a match but you've presented yourself professionally, then you'll have increased your chances of being contacted when a better match opens up.

Don't Prolong the Inevitable
If you pick up signals that the interviewer wants to end the call, don't keep asking questions in an effort to extend the conversation. If you demonstrate you're slow to pick up on cues, it'll detract from you as a candidate.

It Is a Two-Way Street
It's 100 percent safe to assume that everyone is on their best behavior in the interview process. What you see now is as good as it'll ever get. To increase your chances of staying in consideration, be open to discussion and be willing to answer any and all questions. Don't play hard to get, don't expect to be wooed, and don't go on a fishing expedition just for giggles.

Case in point: During an initial phone screen, a candidate said, "Do you see the Education section on my résumé …what do you see?" In those thirteen words, he showed he had a mean streak.

Another case in point: In an introductory call, a candidate said, "If you don't have an executive position open, then we're done." He was needlessly rude, so in a single sentence, he torpedoed any chance of being considered in the future.

From *your* perspective, if a recruiter or hiring manager gets testy with you, just know this is them at their very best, and it'll only get worse from here on in.

Act Like It's Your Dream Job
If you're hesitant, doubtful, or cautious about an opportunity, it'll come across as disinterest or arrogance. To counter this, approach every interview as if it *is* your dream job—that way you'll be more motivated to prepare for each interview and be more engaged in the discussion. If you're not sure the job is for you, pretend it is anyway. You might discover in the last two minutes of an interview that it's actually what you've been waiting for your whole life. If you've been fully engaged throughout the process, you'll have increased your chances of moving forward.

> Show you can work with someone you don't like. Better yet, behave in such a way that they don't even know you don't like them.

Stories from the Trenches…

A job seeker's comment when he took me to task for not presenting him for an interview: "There are few people less accomplished than me."

Preparing for the Interview

What's the Point of the Interview?
An interviewer has just one objective: to decide whether you're a match for the role. *Your* goal is to learn enough about the position and the company to make the right decision should an offer be extended. An interview can be phone, video, or in person, and the preparation is the same for all three.

The Right Mindset
You don't have a real choice until a job offer is made, so view the interview as a sales presentation with you as the product. Even if you're not particularly interested in the job, go through the interview anyway, because…
- It'll be good practice, and it'll give you a chance to hone your interview skills.
- If you do well, you'll have positioned yourself to be considered for other opportunities.
- You might learn something in the interview that changes your perception of the role such that you end up concluding it actually is the opportunity of a lifetime.

Nailing the Conversation
It's all about research and practice, and here are the steps to follow.
- Read every word of the job description. Don't assume anything.
- Think about how your experience matches each requirement.
- Draft some talking points, and come up with a list of questions to ask.
- Go through the hiring company's website, and look at their recent press releases.
- Go to YouTube to see if the company has any product videos—then watch as many as it takes to get a good handle on what they do.
- Go to Glassdoor and see what employees have said about the company; do take comments with a grain of salt, however, as there are always at least three sides to every story (two sides, plus the truth somewhere in the middle).
- Go to the hiring manager's LinkedIn profile, and read it. Don't worry if the hiring manager sees you've peeked—it'll just go to show you're taking time to research.
- Check your contacts to see if you know anyone at the company. If you want to keep your candidacy under the radar, then don't reach out. If you don't mind who knows, then by all means, reach out to anyone who might be able to provide you with additional insight into the organization and who might serve as a reference for you.
- Practice answering and asking questions aloud; the more you practice, the more at ease you'll be in conversation.

Interview Basics
- Smile (even if it's just a phone call, the caller will hear it).
- Make good eye contact during in-person meetings and video calls.
- Sit up straight, even on the phone call.
- Don't chew gum.
- Turn your phone off during the on-site visit.
- If you're kept waiting, don't get aggravated. You don't know what's happening behind the scenes, and your patience will be noted and appreciated.
- Treat everyone as if they're the decision-maker or hiring manager.
- Let the interviewer drive the discussion. If you're speaking and the interviewer starts talking, then you should be quiet and listen.
- Thank people for their time and consideration.

Preparing for the Interview

The Handshake
For time immemorial, the handshake has been the de facto means of greeting or saying goodbye. It's important to have a good solid handshake, so just Google, "how to shake hands with someone" and you'll find a plethora of information.

In 2020, we're in the throes of the COVID-19 pandemic, so handshake protocol has changed due to social distancing requirements. That might change in the future, and we'll just have to wait and see how it all unfolds.

The Rule for Answering Questions
1. Listen to the question.
2. Ask for clarification if you need it.
3. Answer the question.
4. Stop talking.

How to Ask Questions
The interview is most definitely a two-way conversation, so while the interviewer is evaluating you, you're also evaluating the job, the manager, and the company. It's imperative you ask questions so you can capture a full picture of the situation, while also demonstrating your depth of knowledge and experience and how it relates to the company.

Do have a written list of questions to refer to in the interview. Don't just rely on your memory. Never cross-examine the interviewer; just aim to be conversational.

If you're meeting multiple people at the same company, ask similar questions in every interview so you can compare and contrast everyone's answers. If they're not all viewing the role and the goals the same way, it could be an indication they're not consistently defining success, and that will be something you'll need to clarify with the hiring manager before accepting an offer.

What You Should Ask at the End of the Interview
As you sense the interviewer is wrapping up, ask some combination of these questions.
- How close am I to the ideal candidate?
- Is there any experience you feel I might be missing?
- When would you like to have someone onboard?
- What's the next step in the process?
- When should I expect to hear from you?

In any interview, there's a natural back-and-forth to the conversation. The interviewer asks a question, and you answer it. There will be times, though, when the interviewer interrupts you halfway through your response, and the conversation will end up going in a different direction. At the end of the interview, you now have this bucket of information that you wanted to get across but couldn't. To make sure the interviewer has an accurate picture of your skills, you should ask, "How close am I to the ideal candidate?" and "Is there any experience you *feel* I *might* be missing?" If some crucial piece of information got lost in translation, you now have a chance to clarify and adjust the interviewer's perception.

Two keys to success: Write well, and wear clean, polished shoes.

> **Stories from the Trenches...**
>
> A candidate wanted more information about a job and asked, "What does this job in tell?"

Preparing for the Interview

It Only Works if You Practice
The key to success is practicing your questions and answers *out loud* prior to the interview. If you put together a list of questions you found on the internet but then do nothing with them until you ask them in the interview, the interviewer will know you didn't prepare fully and that you're just asking someone else's questions.

If you do practice aloud beforehand, however, you'll make the questions your own and will gain "voice memory." The first few times you speak a question out loud in practice, it'll feel like a tongue twister, but through repetition, you'll be saying the words without even thinking about them. Then, when you ask them in the interview, the words will be second nature, and you'll come across as prepared and polished.

What to Ask When You're Considering Multiple Opportunities
If you're being considered by multiple companies, you're really going to want to know when each company plans on making a decision, and the best way to achieve that is this.

> You: When would you like to have some one onboard?
> The interviewer: We'll make a decision by__
> You: The reason I ask is I'm interviewing with [two] other companies and am trying to gauge the timelines.

This is a professional way to let the interviewer know that other companies are vying for your attention. Your tone should be polite and conversational—and not in any way confrontational or challenging. If the company really wants you on the team, they'll know they have to move quickly. If they can't move fast enough, then at least you'll have an accurate picture of the situation.

What to Have with You during the Phone or Video Interview
Have these things within easy reach.
- The name of the company and interviewer. (How bad would it be if you forgot who you're talking to?)
- The interviewer's phone number so you can call in case you're running late, or if you don't hear from the interviewer as scheduled.
- A copy of your résumé and a copy of the job description.
- Your notes about the company's products and services.
- A notepad, a pen, and a spare pen. (You definitely should plan to take notes during the interview.)
- The list of questions you'd like to ask.
- A handkerchief or a few tissues. (They're way better than your shirt sleeve.)

If it's a video interview, you want the interviewer to focus on you, so make sure you don't have anything distracting around you. To figure out how your surroundings will come across, take a picture of yourself from the perspective of the interviewer, then take a good hard look at what you see. You don't want people, animals, laundry, vacuum cleaners, lighted beer signs, bedroom anything, or an *A Christmas Story* leg lamp in the picture. You get one shot at the interview, so you have to get it right the first time.

> For a video call, make the video screen small, and move it as close to your camera as possible. This'll close the gap between the caller's face and your camera, and will make it appear as if you're looking directly at the camera even though you're actually looking at the caller on the screen.

> **Stories from the Trenches...**
>
> A job seeker emailed that his employer was a start-up company: "We're in tart-up mode."

Preparing for the Interview

Be Respectful of Other People's Time
When you have a phone or video interview, be respectful and make sure the call is your only focus. If you can't devote your full attention, then either eliminate the distraction or reschedule the appointment.

Case in point: I had a scheduled telephone call with an individual who'd lost his job and who was actively conducting a search. When I called at the appointed time, he was cooking lunch for his son and tried to straddle the fence, making a grilled cheese sandwich while also answering my questions. I don't know how the grilled cheese turned out, but he didn't come across on the phone nearly as well as he could have.

To Find Out How You Come Across
Get dressed in your full interview attire, including shoes, accessories, keys, pocketbook, and binder, and then record a practice-run interview. It'll give you fabulous feedback on how you're coming across, plus give you a chance to fine-tune your nonverbal behavior and communication style.

What to Take to the On-Site/In-Person Interview
Take these things with you:
- The name of the interviewer.
- The address and directions to the interview location. To reduce your stress, do a drive-by prior to the interview so you can figure out the best route.
- The interviewer's phone number so you can call in case you're running late.
- Several copies of your résumé.
- Samples of your work…but nothing proprietary or confidential.
- A pen…and a spare.
- A binder. Make sure it's empty of everything except what's pertinent to the interview.
- An energy bar…in case the interview runs over. (You can sneak a snack during a bathroom break.)
- Your recruiter's phone number (if applicable) so you can provide feedback after the interview.
- A handkerchief or a few tissues.

This is my favorite kind of interview binder…there's a pocket on the left for your résumé, and a notepad on the right. It's slim and easy to manage, and you can find them in any office supply store.

> There's a world of difference between, "I can't do it" and "I won't do it." Don't confuse the two.

Stories from the Trenches…

I asked a candidate if there was anyone who had a vote when it came down to her taking a job that required 50 percent travel. She paused a moment then said, "Wow…That's a great question. So what you're really asking is if my boyfriend will bitch if I travel?"

Preparing for the Interview

Ask for the Job
If you genuinely want the job, ask for it, and here are some suggestions.
- Everything I've heard sounds great, and I'm really interested in the position.
- What you're doing here is exciting, and I'd love to be a part of the team.
- From everything you've told me, this is the job I've been hoping for, and I would welcome the chance to join the family.
- When can I start?

It Doesn't Have to Be Your Dream Job
If you've had long stretches of employment with several companies, at least five to ten years in each, don't feel like your next job has to be your dream job. If you have a strong work history already, you can have a short stint or two without people questioning your ability to be a loyal employee.

Consider this employment run. This engineer has two ten-year runs, a short run of two years, and then a six-month stint. The six-month run really doesn't affect him at all because he's already demonstrated loyalty.

July 2019 to Present	Senior Architect, LMO Company	
Jan 2019 to July 2019	Principal Engineer, ABC Company	(This is a 6 month stretch)
Jan 2017 to Jan 2019	Senior Engineer, JKL Company	(This is a 2-year stretch)
Apr 2005 to Nov 2016	Principal Engineer, RST Company	(This is an 11½-year stretch)
Jan 1995 to Mar 2005	Engineer, XYZ Company	(This is a 10-year stretch)

If you've had long tenures at companies, you've earned the latitude to take a transitional job as a bridge to the next role.

Completing the Application
If you're asked to complete an application prior to the interview, then do so.
- Don't leave anything blank. Complete the entire document, especially the Employment section. Don't just put "See résumé" or "Résumé attached."
- Make sure your dates are accurate and that they match up with your résumé and LinkedIn profile.
- Complete all the reference information—don't just put "See attached."

> If you take any kind of large bag (briefcase, oversized shoulder bag, backpack) to the interview, never put it on a desk or table. You've likely had to put it on the ground at some point, so to avoid cross-contamination, put it on a chair or on your lap when you open it.

Stories from the Trenches...

A candidate's comment when he missed our scheduled call: "I'm really good-looking but not really smart."

Preparing for the Interview

Five Feet Is Such a Long Journey

If you've been a hiring manager for years, then you're used to leading discussions and telling people what to do. You won't think it's a big deal to interview because you know how it all works. But even though it's only a few steps from the interviewer's chair to the candidate's chair, there's actually a 180-degree difference in mindset because the responsibility of leading the discussion now belongs to someone else. You have to follow, and that's sometimes tough to do when you're used to leading. Just be mindful of who's in charge of the conversation.

Transportation

If the hiring company arranges for a driver to transport you, treat that driver as if he's part of the interview team. It's safe to assume he'll report back everything you say and do.

If you're driving your own car to the interview, make sure your vehicle is clean inside and out...including the trunk.

If you're flying in, wear professional attire on the plane, and be polite to everyone. You just never know who you'll sit next to. Do not check your luggage. Carry it on and protect it with your life.

Case in point: A candidate flew to South Florida for an interview and landed late evening for an early morning interview the next day. His luggage didn't show up, so on the way to his hotel, he had his taxi driver do a Walmart flyby to get new pants, shirt, and tie. A stressful dilemma, but he demonstrated super problem solving skills!

Dining Etiquette

You will be judged on your table manners, so be vigilant. Here are a few pointers.
- Don't order the most expensive item on the menu.
- Avoid alcohol and carbonated drinks—we don't want any burping or slurring later on.
- Don't drink too much of any beverage.
- Don't be too picky with how you want your food prepared.
- Order an item that can be eaten with a knife and fork.
- Don't overeat.
- Thank your hosts for the meal.
- Don't offer to leave the tip.
- Be polite to the wait staff! Your treatment of those in a service role is a powerful measure of your character.

Be on Time

You must be ready at the appointed time. For a phone interview, get to a quiet location where you won't be disturbed during the call. For the on-site interview, arrive in the parking area twenty to thirty minutes early, then get to the reception desk about ten minutes ahead of time. If you're going to be even one minute late, call ahead and let the interviewer know.

Don't use spam blocker on your email; a lot of recipients won't bother to complete the process, so you run the risk of missing out on conversations.

> **Stories from the Trenches...**
>
> An engineering candidate's ideal job: "To ride dirt bikes and write poetry."

Attire

What to Wear

Attire is all over the place these days, so trying to pinpoint exactly what's appropriate is like trying to herd cats blindfolded in a rainstorm. What might be appropriate in New York will be considered too stuffy in Los Angeles. What's weather-appropriate in Minneapolis will make you melt in Phoenix.

So as soon as anyone mentions an on-site interview, go ahead and ask what appropriate attire might be. By posing this question immediately, you'll come across as a quick thinker. If you forget to ask it, just email a note as soon as it comes to mind. If you never think to ask, or if you're just going to wing it, here's a guideline.

	East coast	Midwest	Southcentral	West coast
Major corporation C-suite	Formal business attire	Formal business attire	Formal business attire	Formal business attire or high-end business casual
Major corporation Executive level	Formal business attire	Formal business attire	Formal business attire	Formal business attire or high-end business casual
Major corporation Mid level—Sales	Formal business attire	Formal business attire	Formal business attire	Formal business attire or high-end business casual
Major corporation Mid-level Engineering	Formal business attire or high-end business casual	High-end business casual	High-end business casual	High-end business casual
Major corporation Entry level	Formal business attire	High-end business casual	High-end business casual	High-end business casual
Regional or local company	Formal business attire or high-end business casual	Formal business attire or high-end business casual	Formal business attire or high-end business casual	High-end business casual
Retail company	High-end business casual	High-end business casual	High-end business casual	High-end business casual
Building or manufacturing company	Casual or work clothes	Casual or work clothes	Casual or work clothes	Casual or work clothes

If you're really worried about what to wear, you can swing by the employee parking lot at quitting time and see what most people have on, then decide from there. If the interviewer tells you, "We're really casual here," then go with high-end business casual. When in doubt, go with formal business attire. If you show up in a suit and tie but it turns out the atmosphere is more relaxed, you can always take the jacket off. If you show up in slacks and a polo shirt but everyone else is in suit and tie, you're up the creek without a paddle. If in doubt, dress like you're going to meet a VIP…because you are.

Once you've had one on-site interview and have seen what people are wearing, you'll be able to decide whether to be a bit less formal the next time or to stay with your original attire. Standards change like the wind, though; what might be formal business attire today might be different in five years, so google the definition of the different types of attire, and then go with your gut.

> On every trip to the restroom, check your reflection. Is your fly unzipped, is your shirttail hanging out through your fly, is your skirt or dress tucked into your underwear, is there food or lipstick on your teeth, has your mascara/eyeliner run, is there dandruff on your shoulders?

Attire

What I Can Tell You about Attire
Although selecting attire is a bit of a stab in the dark, I can without any hesitation tell you this:
- Make sure your clothes are clean and nicely ironed. Don't just iron the part of the clothing that shows (for example, iron the *whole* shirt—not just the collar, cuffs and front).
- Clean and polish your shoes.
- Get a haircut, and make sure any facial hair is neatly trimmed. Check nose and ear hair, and those eyebrows!
- Check that all buttons are attached. If a button is hanging by a thread, sew it back in place.
- Make sure your clothes fit properly and don't gap anywhere. No one wants to look at your chest hair, bra, or belly button.
- Look in the mirror and check your front, side, and rear views to make sure everything fits properly.
- Pull your pants up. Waistbands should be at the waist…not at crotch level.
- Trim your nails and make sure your hands are clean.
- Use deodorant, and avoid pungent colognes or perfumes.
- Don't wear brand-new shoes. Instead, wear shoes that are already broken in and comfortable.
- Don't wear flip-flops…even if they are bedazzled and match your toenail polish.
- Don't wear a baseball cap.
- Make sure your underwear doesn't show through your clothing.

Case in point: At a trade show, I was talking with someone who had dandruff on his shoulders and eyebrows that looked like shrubs. It was all I could do not to brush the dandruff off his jacket, and I was utterly transfixed watching those eyebrows bob up and down.

Why You Should Adhere to Standards
The earlier you are in your career, the more likely you are to argue that you should be allowed to dress as you want. Unfortunately, life's just not that easy, and if you want to be able to support yourself (and a family at some point), then you have to earn a decent and consistent wage. To accomplish this, you need longevity with an employer. To remain employed over the long haul, you have to adhere to your employer's generally accepted guidelines for behavior, work ethic, punctuality, attendance…and dress code.

Like it or not, people will judge you by what you wear, and if you look sloppy, they'll draw the conclusion that your work must be sloppy too.

If you love body art and want to work in a tattoo parlor, go for it. If you're aiming to work in an office, then you need to wear appropriate office attire and adhere to generally accepted standards.

> **Stories from the Trenches…**
>
> The neutral-colored-underwear rule is a result of my own mistake. I was taking clients to dinner at a trade show and had made a mad dash to my hotel to change into more casual attire before meeting my group for the walk to the restaurant. We were halfway to the restaurant when I realized my bright underwear was shining like a beacon through my white slacks. I was mortified. To this day, I still remember exactly the point along that walk when the realization hit me, and I still remember exactly who was in that group.

Questions You Can Ask

Inquiring Minds Want to Know

Do have a list of questions written out and ready to go and, as you make your way through all the discussions, get enough information to answer these questions.

- Why is the job open? Is it a new role or a backfill? If it's a backfill, what happened to the last person?
- How long has the job been open? If it's been open an extended period of time, what's the reason for that?
- If it's an existing role, have there been any recent adjustments to the responsibilities?
- Does the job description match what the manager says he's looking for?
- What does the situation look like now, and what does the manager want done immediately? In the next six months? In the next three to five years?
- Are the goals reasonable…are they-pie-in-the-sky, challenging-but-achievable, or a-walk-in-the-park?
- What resources are available to achieve these goals?
- How will success be measured?
- What's been done already to achieve the goals, and what was the outcome?
- Are there any major obstacles or challenges that might hinder the achievement of these goals?
- Is there anyone internally who wants the role, and are they currently being considered?
- How big is the team or department?
- Who's the manager, and what's his/her personality and managerial style?
- What's the team like? Are there varying personalities, or is the group more homogeneous?
- What's a typical day like?
- What's the corporate culture like, and how do the different departments interact with each other?
- If you do well and prove your stripes, are there additional responsibilities that can be earned?
- Is there any additional education that might make you more successful in the role, and does the company provide funding for that?
- What's included in the benefits package?
- Can you see your prospective work area?

> **Stories from the Trenches…**
>
> A conversation with an account manager I'd found on LinkedIn. I'd called to ask if he was interested in considering a new job opportunity:
> Account Manager: "I appreciate that you have a job to do, but I'd like to request that you take our company off your call list. What you're doing is poaching, and if you call anyone at our company again, I'll lodge a complaint."
> Me: "With who?"
> Account Manager: "I'll call your company and complain to your boss!"
> Me: "Well…I own the company."
> Account Manager: "Well, how would you like it if I called up your company and tried to steal your employees?"
> Me: "But we've only got three people here."
> Account Manager: "Well, maybe there's a reason for that!"
>
> Well played, friend, well played.

Questions You Can Ask

Questions for a Start-Up Company
Start-ups can be risky, so make sure you do enough research to weigh all the pros and cons. Here's what to find out.
- How old is the company, and how is it funded?
- What's the situation with capital, and how many months can it survive without additional investment?
- Do they hold the patents?
- Is the product solution agnostic?
- How many successful installations or implementations are there?
- How many referenceable customers are there in the United States? Elsewhere in the world?
- How easy is it to replicate the technology? What measures have been taken to protect the product from being copied?
- Why is the technology going to be in demand? What will make the technology successful?
- Where they are now in the development phase, and what's planned for the next three to five years?
- What's the target market?
- Who are their competitors, and how does the competition differ?
- How do they go to market?
- Can you see a product demonstration?
- What's the executive team's background in this field? Have they worked together before in another venture and how did that venture turn out?
- What's the ultimate exit strategy? Will the company be positioned for sale, or will they expand?
- Would equity be part of the offer?

Active Listening
Sometimes it's not the question you ask but the follow-up question that gets you the better intel. For this, you have to listen well and not jump to conclusions. Focus on what's being said and not just on what you want to say next.

> If you're wearing a dress or a skirt and you bend over at the hips but you don't bend your knees at the same time, just know that everyone behind you is going to see your knickers. This accidental flash is most common when the wearer is getting into a taxi van or hotel shuttle and has to bend over to get into the vehicle.
> FYI: If you're wearing pantyhose with that skirt or dress, please wear underwear as well. There are some things you just can't un-see.

Stories from the Trenches...

A candidate said: "If I accept the offer that is on the table from this other company, I can always retract it before starting to work if *your* client were to offer me something more favorable."
After he was a no-show for an interview with my client, he said: "I'm sure they'll let bygones be bygones once they meet me."

Questions You Might Be Asked

It's not possible to plan for every single interview question, but by reading through examples and practicing answers, you'll be more relaxed and prepared for the interview. There are a plethora of websites offering lists, so troll through and cherry-pick what you like best. Think of applicable situations where you really excelled, then use the interviewer's questions as a springboard to talk about those success stories.

In general, interviewers will ask open-ended questions, so you should provide detail in your reply. Don't go with just one-word answers unless you know for sure that's what's expected.

What interests you most about this position?
Use the opportunity to demonstrate your knowledge of the company and the role, and answer the question in terms of what you could bring to the organization.

What are your career goals?
Answer in terms of both short- and long-term goals. And be realistic.

What are you doing to achieve your goals?
Many people have a wish list of goals but don't do anything to get closer to them, so make sure you have something concrete to say that highlights what you're doing today to get you where you want to be.

Why did you leave your previous employer?
Package this reply carefully. Don't give too much detail—just keep it brief, and don't in any way trash your former boss or employer.

What did you like most and least about your previous job?
What you liked most can include a strong teamwork atmosphere, high level of creativity, and challenging projects. What you liked least should be situations that most people want to avoid, like a company merger/buyout/outsourcing, a non-cohesive team, or an ever-changing territory or customer list.

What are you looking for in another job?
The safest responses are to focus on wanting to gain responsibilities, experience, or a career trajectory that maybe hasn't been available to you up to now, or to talk about wanting a more stable environment.

Are you applying for any other jobs?
Here are some possible responses:
   Not actively looking: "I haven't been looking but was approached by a recruiter, and the opportunity seemed so compelling I had to put my name in for consideration."
   Passively looking: "I really like my current job, but there's not much opportunity for growth, so I'm open to a new challenge."
   Actively looking: "I'm currently interviewing with [two] other companies and hope to make a decision within a month or so." (Or whatever time frame is appropriate.)

> Interviewers will deliberately interrupt you to see how well you can adjust to a new topic, or how well you can get back on topic.

Stories from the Trenches...

Seen on LinkedIn: "I do better in person."

Questions You Might Be Asked

What areas are you interested in?
The interviewer wants to find out if you've taken inventory of your strengths and weaknesses, and if you've matched them up reasonably with a career path.

How do you make decisions?
One approach is to explain that you research a problem and try to gather as much information as possible, then make the best decision with the information you have. Admit that you're not right 100 percent of the time but that when you are wrong, you're willing to admit it and work to learn from your mistakes.

Can you give an example of how you failed at something, and how did you recover?
This is a powerful question and can really shed light on how you view failure. The best reply I've ever heard was, "I was in a high-level math class in university but didn't study that first week, got behind, and never caught up. I stayed in the class even though I knew I would fail, then I retook it the next semester and made an A. The semester after that, I was hired to be the teacher's assistant for the class."

It's not so much the failure itself, it's how you dealt with it that is a measure of your character.

What causes you to lose your temper?
Everybody has a boiling point, so don't say you never lose your temper—it's just not believable. Just pick something safe and reasonable that everyone hates, like blame shifting, office backstabbing, or gossiping.

What are your greatest accomplishments?
Be ready to recite one or two stories that demonstrate your strong capabilities or achievements that tie in with the job description.

What kind of worker are you?
Talk about being willing to take on a challenge and add that you are collaborative and a team player, but also can work solo when needed.

Are you willing to relocate?
Location of the role should be listed in the job description, so if a move is required, check with everyone in your household who'll be affected by a move. Do this early in the process to save time.

Case in point: One candidate assured me his wife desperately wanted to move from Atlanta to Memphis to be closer to family and that I'd be on their Christmas card list if I could get them home. He ended up getting a great offer but declined it when his eighth-grade daughter, who didn't want to leave her friends, dug in her heels and persuaded them to stay put. Teenage girls rule!

Describe your past work experiences: What were the high points? What were the problems?
Everyone has challenges, but the interviewer isn't so much interested in what the problem actually was but more in how you handled the situation and what you learned from it.

> Avoid phrases that might make you come across as passive aggressive: as I just said, as I already mentioned, obviously, as it says in my résumé, if you'll remember.

Stories from the Trenches...

An email from a candidate who'd just accepted a job offer: "Haven't received the drug screen instructions yet. Been holding my pee for two days now."

Questions You Might Be Asked

What lessons have you learned from your past work experiences?
The interviewer wants to hear about those "educational opportunities" you've had along the way. If you haven't made mistakes, you're either deluding yourself or you haven't been working hard enough.

Why did you choose your particular field of work?
Most people had no clue what they wanted to be when they grew up and ended up accidentally falling into a job that turned into a career. And it's totally okay to say that.

What personal characteristics are necessary for success in your chosen field?
The interviewer wants to know that you're well-grounded in your outlook and that you understand what it takes to succeed in your field. Have you taken inventory of your own strengths and weaknesses? How do you react when the going gets tough? And what are you doing to improve?

What jobs have you enjoyed the most? The least? Why?
Make sure your reply overlaps with the job duties of the role for which you're being considered.

What are the disadvantages of your chosen field? How have you handled them, and how will you handle them in the future?
This is another of those questions where the interviewer wants to gauge how you handle issues, so your answer should show how you can rise above difficulties.

What have you done that shows your initiative and willingness to work?
The interviewer wants to make sure you work well independently and won't need to be micromanaged.

Describe your present job responsibilities. Which are the most difficult and why?
Be careful with this one. Keep your reply brief, and be neutral so you won't come across as a complainer.

What do you know about our company and this position?
If you've done your homework, you'll soar through this question. If you've chosen to wing it and not research the company, this question could torpedo your chances.

Case in point: In 1986, I landed an interview with Sonoco Products, a global manufacturing company. I had less than twenty-four hours to prepare and didn't have time to go to the library to read through annual reports, so I had to wing it. My last interview of the day was with a VP. He asked me what I knew about Sonoco, and I replied that it was a national company. I couldn't have highlighted my lack of preparation any more than I did, and I shot myself so badly in both feet I had to crawl out of that meeting. Needless to say, they didn't pick me.

FYI...it is okay to have your notes on the company with you in the interview, and you certainly can refer to them; just don't read them verbatim.

How would you describe your personality? How would your associates describe you?
Focus your answer around being loyal, hardworking, and a go-getter; showing initiative; being good at problem-solving; researching problems to get a better understanding; being great with customers; being easy to manage; and being a resource for coworkers by being helpful, cooperative, punctual, and willing to do what's necessary to get the job done.

Don't describe anyone as a psycho...no matter how accurate a description it might be.

Questions You Might Be Asked

Describe what qualities you like in a supervisor.
Here, you can list things like encouraging teamwork, letting employees take the initiative, and encouraging them to take on additional responsibility or continue their education.

What are the biggest frustrations in your career?
Keep your answer brief and neutral. Two options to talk about are maybe a lack of resources or little opportunity to advance your career, because most interviewers will be able to relate to both.

What might your present company or department do to become more successful?
This is a trick question, and the interviewer wants to see if you'll take the bait and obliterate your current company or boss. Keep it neutral so you don't come across as bitter.

What elements are important for your job satisfaction?
Talk about what motivates you. If you're interviewing for a sales position, then achieving quota goals and having higher earnings potential should be in your top three. If the position is technical, then talk about new technology or project completion.

What's the best thing that ever happened to you?
This is a chance for you to be introspective and talk about a decision you've made that's impacted your career.

What's been the most pivotal moment in your career?
This is a great chance to talk about a major difficulty or obstacle you had to overcome, and how it changed your trajectory.

What's the worst thing that ever happened to you, work-wise?
This is a way for you to show how you handle adversity.

What's a recent problem you weren't able to solve?
This is a way for you to show how you handle disappointment, and then adapt.

What's something you learned recently that surprised you?
Interviewers want to hire people who are open to learning, so this is a great way to highlight a willingness to grow.

What would you like to have accomplished in your present job but haven't? Why not?
If you've been held up by a lack of resources, it's okay to say that…just don't be negative or derogatory. Again, no trash talk.

In your present job, what accomplishments are you most proud of? What was your best idea?
Give one or two examples of how you've contributed, and include how you've shown initiative.

What's the biggest risk you've ever taken, and how did it turn out?
Of primary interest, here, is how you calculated and managed the risk, navigated the decision-making process, and adjusted when things didn't go as planned.

Questions You Might Be Asked

When can you start?
This is a trick question. Prospective employers will predict how you'll treat them based on the level of courtesy you extend to your current employer. If you're currently employed and say you can start immediately, you've demonstrated you're not a loyal employee. It's best to say you'd like to give two weeks' notice but will be able to start earlier if your current employer says it's okay to leave sooner.

The Sneak-Attack Three-Part Question
Some interviewers will toss out a three-part question, and you'll be judged on the completeness of your response. Here are some examples.

> 1. What do you like about your current job?
> 2. What do you like about your boss?
> 3. What would your boss say about you?

> 1. What part of your current job do you dislike?
> 2. Does that affect your performance?
> 3. How do you adjust?

A trick to remembering all three parts of the question is to repeat them back to the interviewer first, and to hold up fingers to emphasize the one…two…three count. As you answer the first part of the question, hold up the one-finger count. When you get to the second part of the question, hold up the two-finger count. When you get to the third part of the question, hold up the three-finger count. It'll help keep you on track.

Is It Okay to Say, "I Don't Know"?
It absolutely is okay to not have an answer, but follow up with, "Can I find out and get back with you?" If you do say this, make a note right then and there in the interview, and make sure you follow up as soon as possible after the interview.

What if You Need Time to Think?
If an interviewer stumps you with a question, answer with, "That's a great question." It'll buy you an extra few moments to gather your thoughts and come up with a response. Don't use this for every question, though, as it'll be annoying and the interviewer will be crawling the walls by the end of the meeting.

Don't Overuse the Interviewer's Name
Using the interviewer's name at the beginning of every answer will be a sure way to get you kicked out of consideration. You wouldn't do that in an everyday conversation with a friend, so don't do it in the interview.

There's a time to be flexible and there's a time to be rigid. But there's never a time to be rude.

> **Stories from the Trenches…**
>
> Seen on LinkedIn: "Born at a very young age. Following my dream and painting the silence with sound."

Questions You Might Be Asked

A Few Final Thoughts
- If you're in a panel interview, jot down the names of the interviewers on your note pad, and write them in the order in which they're seated. A quick glance down at your notes will remind you of each person's name.
- It's not so much *what* you say but *how* you say it that is the key to success.
- Never use the term *work-life balance;* consider using *work-life integration* instead.
- If you're in sales—you must ask closing questions. If you don't close the interviewer, you won't close a customer.
- Keep your career aspirations realistic, and don't act like you want the hiring manager's job.

> **Don't minimize what you do, and never say, "I'm just a…teacher…secretary…cashier." You have much to offer the world, so don't sell yourself short.**

Stories from the Trenches…

Email from a candidate who didn't match the job criteria: "Thanks Jane, perhaps a little more research would help you fill the role more effectively, or it may be that your skill set is not a match to recruit candidates for this type of role. Perhaps you misunderstood since you do not seem to possess such marketing and communication skills or the aptitude to see that my background clearly reflects my work. I would be interested to know how much time and money such assumptions have cost the company you represent, you clearly are not suited to effectively recruit talent in this capacity. Best of luck!"

Hmmmmm. I don't think she really meant those best-of-luck wishes.

Putting Lipstick on a Pig

How do you tell the truth when the truth is kind of ugly? The answer is you think about it ahead of time and practice speaking it out loud in order to take the emotion out of the equation. This allows you to be polite, tactful, and neutral.

The truth	A non-emotional perspective
My boss is a total nutjob and I can't stand his guts, and if I have to spend one more day working in this crazy place then I won't be held responsible for the Reply-All email I'm gonna send out!	My boss is having some personal issues, and the entire team is under duress as a result. I don't see the situation changing any time soon, so I'm open to a new opportunity.
I have 20 years with the company, but now the owner's twenty-something son has become my boss and all he does is play video games in his office. Five times a day he stomps out of his office and yells "Get busy!" and then goes back to Minecraft.	The owner's son just graduated from university, and he's now managing my department and is being groomed to take over the company. The company culture is changing, so I'm open to a new opportunity.
My company just got bought out, and I'm terrified I'll lose my job. I have kids and a mortgage. How am I going to survive if they fire me?	My company was just acquired and future job security is uncertain, so I'm actively conducting a search.
A newly hired VP has a potty-mouth, and he drops the F-bomb every other sentence. I just can't live like this.	A new VP is taking the team in a new direction and our group's dynamics are changing to be less team oriented, so I'm actively conducting a search.
The Sales Manager hired his neighbor and gave this new guy all my best accounts, so now I'm making less money *and* having to train this guy to handle the customers I developed.	My boss hired his neighbor as a sales rep and has split my account base with the new rep. This has really reduced my earnings potential, so I'm open to a new opportunity.
They doubled the cost of our health insurance so I can't afford to work here anymore, but I cannot be without health insurance because my child has a debilitating health problem.	The cost of our benefits have just gone up and it's drastically reduced my take-home income, so I'm actively conducting a search.
I'm being bullied by co-workers and my boss won't stand up for me.	The work environment can be somewhat toxic and I don't see it improving, so I'm actively conducting a search for a new opportunity.

> **Some employment situations are so painful it just seems impossible to come up with a neutral reason for leaving. If that's the case, try writing out what you want to say, then refine the wording until there's no emotion left. To hear how it sounds, speak it out loud. Practice it over and over until you can say it in a neutral tone.**

The Elephant in the Room

Be Direct

If you feel there's an issue that could torpedo your chances of getting the job, then tactfully address the issue head-on. Don't be bashful about it. Just point to the elephant in the room (or issue) and ask if it's a showstopper. A few examples.

> **The issue:** The job description lists 75 percent travel, the recruiter has said it's only 50 percent, and your family situation is such that you can only accommodate up to about 50 percent.
>
> **The question to ask:** "The job description lists 75 percent travel, but the recruiter mentioned it's only around 50 percent. What will the travel likely be? Are there spikes up to 75 percent at certain times of the year, or will it always be at that level?"

> **The issue:** Your current salary is much higher than the range you've been quoted.
>
> **The question to ask:** "You mentioned that the current salary range is $100K to $110K with around $130K after the bonus, but my salary right now is $150K, and last year I earned $180K. Has the salary range adjusted at all?"

> **The issue:** The company was recently acquired and has been downsizing, and you want to know how secure your job will be long term if you join the team.
>
> **The question to ask:** "The company was recently acquired, and I've talked to a couple of long-time industry colleagues who were recently caught up in a downsizing here. Is there a chance that, if I were to join the team, this role might be cut at some point in the future?"

The key to handling any elephant in the room is to point to it and talk about it. If the issue is actually a showstopper, then you've just saved yourself time and effort continuing down an interview process that's a waste of time. If the issue really isn't an issue at all, then you can breathe easy and stop worrying about it. Either way, it's healthier to bring the issue to the forefront than to try and ignore it.

💡 **No matter what happens...get up, dress up, and show up.**

> **Stories from the Trenches...**
>
> A thirty-two-year-old self-proclaimed entrepreneur said he didn't want to be the person spending seventy hours a week draining his energy and soul working in an office.

Don't Use the "R" Word

Retirement
A mid-fifties senior executive had lost his job in a downsizing. He was a perfect match for a VP of Sales role we had open, but he tripped up when he used the "R" word and said during the interview, "I'm not ready to retire."

Because he said he wasn't ready to retire, he inferred that he must have seriously pondered whether it was actually a possibility. The company president wanted to hire someone who could eventually take over her role, so when the candidate said the "R" word, that gave a strong indication he might not be around for as long as the president needed him to be.

A Better Approach
If you have taken a retirement package from your company, use the word "severance" instead, and say that you took a voluntary severance package and are now conducting a job search.

How Much Runway Is Left?
A legitimate question in a hiring manager's mind will be how long a new hire will likely stay in the role. If the role that's open actually tracks to a higher-level position, then the question will be whether the new hire will be around long enough to a) move into the higher role, and b) remain in the higher-level role long enough for the company to reap the benefits of its investment.

If you're, say, sixty years old and have been in the workforce for thirty-five years, and your plan is to work until your late sixties, then the recruiter or hiring manager will really want to know how long you'll likely stay around. The question might be, "The hiring manager is looking for someone who has at least a fifteen-year runway so that the new hire can accomplish the goals set forth now, plus move up into the next role. Does that time frame match with what you have in mind?"

If it doesn't fit what you're aiming for, then say so, and back away from the table gracefully. It's far better to halt the process than to drag yourself (and the hiring manager) through the weeds for a role that doesn't make sense for you.

Age Discrimination
Age discrimination happens all the time, and people can stamp their feet and shake their fists, but it won't change the fact that it does happen. If you sense that a company won't consider you because of your age, why would you want to work for them in the first place? By showing you they don't value your experience, they've done you a favor, and you should thank your lucky stars you've seen it early and can just wash that dust off your shoes.

Your job is on loan. Your career is your own.

Stories from the Trenches...

A candidate noted that, "being creative doesn't mean you recreate a Picasso; it means you have the clarity to see all the possibilities plus all the consequences, and then to identify the best course of action to achieve the goal."

After the Interview

Post-interview
1. If you're being represented by a third-party recruiter, then check in with your recruiter to debrief.
2. Send a thank-you note to the interviewer. (More information on this on the next page.)
3. Record your thoughts about the role, the hiring manager, the team, and the company. This is particularly important if you're interviewing with multiple companies, because situations can all start to blend together after a while. If you're just going by memory, you run the risk of not remembering things accurately and then making a mistake.
4. Make a list of any new questions that have come to mind, plus relist those questions you wanted to get answered but didn't.
5. Put a reminder in your calendar to follow up with the recruiter or hiring manager to get a decision.

When to Check Back
If you asked the closing questions during the interview, you might already have an idea of when a decision will be made and when you should expect to hear back. If you've not heard back by the deadline, then follow up on the day specified. Do not check in earlier than this, because it'll indicate you don't listen. Sending a thank-you note will suffice in the meantime.

If you didn't get a straight answer to your closing questions (or if you didn't ask any at all), then you should email in three to five business days. If you don't get a response to your first check-in, wait another four to five business days, and either email again or telephone. But don't do both.

The follow-up can be tricky, but if you come up with a set process for yourself, it'll take the emotion out of the equation and make it easier to handle.

If You Don't Want to Continue
If you decide at any point in the process that you no longer want to be considered for the role, then you must let the interviewer or recruiter know. Don't ghost—that's just rude and immature. Instead, be brave and either call or email saying you appreciate being considered but don't feel it's the right role for you. Here's an example.

> Dear _____
> Thank you so much for your time and consideration for the role of _____, but I feel I must withdraw from the interview process at this time. I wish you all the best!
> Regards

It's tough to recover from a bad first impression, so be vigilant at all times.

Stories from the Trenches...

I was conducting a search for an entry-level candidate and was phone screening a new college grad. Her voice was muffled, so I said it sounded like she was in a bucket. She said, "Well, I don't know why, I'm just lying down." I morphed into mother-hen mode and told her to sit up straight and to never do that again. She really wasn't the right person for the role, but her résumé was in bad shape, and I just couldn't walk away without helping her, so I scheduled another conversation to walk her through some changes. I called her at that next appointed time, and she sounded muffled again. I asked her if she was lying down. There was this really long pause, and I heard a lot of rustling. Then she said, "Ummmm...no."

Thank-You Notes

You Must Be Timely
Definitely email a thank-you note, and make sure it goes out as close to the day of the interview as possible. It's much better to say, "Thank you for your time today" than it is to say, "Thank you for your time last week."

If you snail mail a thank-you note via the US Post Office, make sure it's in addition to your emailed version. If you just snail mail, there will be too much of a delay in getting your note to the recipient, so you may be disqualified from consideration because you didn't follow up in a timely manner.

What to Say
There's no need to summarize your background or the interview. Just keep your email brief, such that the interviewer can read it on the cell phone while walking to or from the elevator. Don't attempt to resell yourself. If you didn't get it right in the interview, you likely won't change anyone's mind now. Since most people don't send thank-you notes anymore, the mere fact that you actually sent one will win you points. The interviewer may not remember what you said but will remember that you bothered to email. Here's a sample thank-you note.

> Dear___
> Thank you so much for your time this afternoon; it was a pleasure meeting you and learning about the opportunity at XYZ Company. I'm very interested in the position and would welcome the chance to move forward in the process. If there's any additional information I can provide, don't hesitate to let me know.
> I look forward to hearing back from you regarding the opportunity.
> Regards,

Aim for a style of communication that's relaxed, focused, and quietly confident. Push without pressuring.

Thanking Multiple Interviewers at the Same Company
If you interviewed with several people on the same visit, then it's okay to send a note to all of them at the same time. Here's an example.

> Good morning!
> Thank you all so much for your time yesterday; it was a pleasure meeting you and learning about the opportunity at XYZ Company. I'm very interested in the position and would welcome the chance to move forward in the process. If there's any additional information I can provide, don't hesitate to let me know.
> I look forward to hearing back from you regarding the opportunity.
> Regards

During the interview, aim to gather the email address of everyone with whom you interviewed. For more sample thank-you notes, a simple Google search will yield more than you can count.

Stories from the Trenches...

Listed on résumés: "There's a low probability of mutual amourment," and, "my next transgression is…"

Why You May Not Get the Job

Rejection Is Part of the Process
Not being selected for an interview or a job doesn't mean you're worth any less than what you were before you started; it just means the decision-maker didn't feel you were right for the role. To maintain your sanity, draw a bold circle around every interview process in order to keep everything compartmentalized, and don't allow a disappointment from one company to bleed into any other interview process.

Here are two responses I received from executive candidates when they weren't moved forward in a process. The first candidate was never considered again. The second one definitely was.

> In the past I ran a 1/2 billion dollar business...but if that's not enough for your President...it seems like he's made up his mind. ✗

> If the criteria changes, I would be interested. And if you find something that you feel is a better fit please reach out. Appreciate your time. Best regards. ✓

Factors You Can Control
If you feel things didn't go well in an interview, do some critical thinking and see if it might be any of these reasons.
- Timidity or a hesitant approach.
- Lack of professionalism because you were too relaxed.
- Arrogance or self-absorption.
- Lack of goals and ambition.
- Indecision about the job. Hesitation is often misinterpreted as arrogance or disinterest, so be aware!
- Lack of enthusiasm about working for the company.
- Poor personal appearance.
- Unrealistic salary demands.
- Greater interest in pay than in the job itself.
- Inability to express ideas.
- Lack of preparation prior to the interview.
- Lack of interest in the employer and the type of job available.
- Directions not followed.
- Attitude of "What can you do for me?"

> Even if you're not in a managerial role, you still have to manage your relationships with other people, so learn to manage in four directions; upward to management, sideways to peers, downward to subordinates, and outward to customers and vendors.

Stories from the Trenches...

An awesome header on LinkedIn: "Retired and liberated, but always willing to help."

Why You May Not Get the Job

Factors You Can't Control
There are some things over which you have zero control.
- The interview went perfectly, but you're overqualified.
- There was another candidate whose experience was a closer match.
- Your compensation requirements are higher than the budgeted range.
- An internal candidate surfaced at the last minute, so all external candidates were sidelined.
- The job was unexpectedly put on hold.

Whatever happens, just keep moving forward.

Is It Possible to Be Too Formal?
Mostly the issue is to get candidates to be less relaxed and to amp up on the professionalism, but every now and then, there's been a candidate on the other end of the spectrum who's been too formal.

Case in point: A candidate had just moved from India to Canada and was conducting a search for a sales role—he already had six years of sales experience in India and was fabulously qualified. He really impressed the hiring manager in the initial phone screen, but he came across as being too formal, so we weren't sure he'd fit with the team. The candidate had approached the interview with the same level of protocol that had been appropriate in India, but this was Canada, eh, and so much more relaxed! I coached him to skip the formality and fast-forward to a more professionally friendly style. His new more-relaxed approach worked like a charm...he nailed the on-site interview and got the offer!

Tomorrow Is Always Another Day
If you're not selected for the job but you did impress the interviewer, you'll have increased your chances of being considered for another role down the road. Plus, every conversation is a chance to tweak your approach, so you can improve the next time around.

They Might Circle Back to You
If you're the runner-up candidate, it might not be over. The lead candidate might take a counteroffer and stay with his company, or fail the drug screen, or have rotten references. You just never know what'll happen. So be professional from start to finish, and you'll be well positioned to be pulled back into consideration.

You can't change the past, but you do have complete control over what you do next.

> **Stories from the Trenches...**
>
> I'd failed to tell a general manager candidate what interview attire to wear and called him right before he boarded his flight to the interview to apologize for failing to give him the information. He said, "I've got it covered...I've got a T-shirt, bib overalls, and some muddy work boots packed, and I haven't shaved in three days. I'm all good!"

Why You May Not Get the Job

But I Don't Wanna Be Second Choice
Don't feel put out if a company comes back to you when the lead candidate didn't work out. If you're second, or even third, choice, you'll be in great company.

    Harrison Ford was third choice to play Indiana Jones in *Raiders of the Lost Ark*.
    Tom Hanks was second choice to play Jim Lovell in *Apollo 13*.
    Arnold Schwarzenegger was second choice for *The Terminator*.
    And all three of them laughed, and laughed, and laughed…all the way to the bank.

Rejecting Rejection
One candidate with an excellent wit said he refused to be rejected and had this form letter ready to send out.

> [Date Today]
> Dear [Interviewer's Name]
> Thank you for your letter of [date]. After careful consideration, I regret to inform you that I am unable to accept your refusal to offer me employment with your firm.
>
> This year I have been particularly fortunate in receiving an unusually large number of rejection letters. With such a varied and promising field of candidates, it is impossible for me to accept all refusals.
>
> Despite [Company Name]'s outstanding qualification and previous experience in rejecting candidates, I find that your rejection does not meet with my needs at this time. Therefore, I will initiate employment with your firm immediately following vacation. I look forward to seeing you then.
>
> Best of luck in rejecting future candidates.
> Sincerely

💡 *If you claim to be a hunter but you can't point to the kill you brought home, you're not a hunter.*

Stories from the Trenches…

On an early-morning flight, an executive was seated next to a young man who'd just graduated from college and who was on his way to an interview. When breakfast was served, the young man opened up a jelly packet, and it burst open all over his shirt. The executive saved the day, though, and swapped shirts with the young man. If that young man had been faced with the interview question, "What's a recent stressful situation you've experienced?" he certainly could have started out with, "Weeelllll, funny you should ask… you won't believe what happened at breakfast this morning."

The Non-Compete Agreement

They're Now Part of the Fabric

The non-compete agreement is now commonplace for an employee who has access to customers or proprietary information. The agreement is designed to prevent an employee from going to a competitor and using knowledge of the prior employer to the advantage of the new employer.

In order to be fair to both employer and employee, a non-compete agreement should protect the former employer's interests while also allowing a former employee to make a living elsewhere. A lot of non-compete agreements actually list the companies deemed competitors, so you're aware of your future options.

If you're conducting a job search and have a non-compete that's still in effect, then be up front with the recruiter or hiring manager. They'll likely ask you for a copy so their in-house counsel can confirm they can actually hire you, so be prepared to send it over.

If you're asked to sign a non-compete at any time, have an attorney review it before signing.

If it's a broad agreement with no list of competitors, then request the agreement be amended to include those competitors you'll be prohibited from joining within the given time period. If the response is, "Everyone's our competitor," that's a symptom of a dysfunctional or unreasonable corporate culture, and you might want to think twice about joining that team.

If you already work for the company and your boss shows up one day and demands you sign a non-compete, you should definitely have an attorney review it first.

In exchange for signing a non-compete, you can ask for a severance payout that equals the time period of the non-compete. This is easier to gain if you're an executive or if you have a rare skill set that's in high demand.

If you are currently under a non-compete, then abide by the terms. It's the honorable thing to do.

If you don't ask, you don't get.

Stories from the Trenches...

I called a sales rep to see if he was open to a new opportunity. This was our conversation:
Me: "This is Jane Snipes." (I deliberately didn't say I was a recruiter because I couldn't tell if he had me on speakerphone or not, and I didn't want to blurt out that I was a recruiter in case his boss was within earshot. My next question would have been to ask if I was on speaker. If not, I'd have filled him in on my being a recruiter and the nature of my call...but I didn't get that chance.)
Him: "What's this regarding?"
Me: "I'm calling about sales in New Jersey and New York." (Again...I'm still waiting for a chance to see if I'm on speakerphone.)
Him: "It's not a good time...I'm on vacation."

Hmmmm...he's in sales but thought it was okay to be rude to what could have been a prospective customer with money to spend with his company. Not a great approach.

The Offer

What to Find Out
As you go through the interviewing process, you'll pick up details about benefits along the way. Once the offer is extended, you should double-check your notes to make sure you have all the requisite information about the role and the benefits. If some piece of information is missing, then add it to your list of questions.

Of Primary Importance
- What's the official title and what's the base salary?
- Is there variable compensation? If yes, is it in the form of a bonus or commission?
    - Can you have a copy of the plan?
    - Is the goal based on individual, group, or company performance, or some combination of the three?
    - What have the goals been for the last few years? Were they achieved?
    - What are the goals now, and have they changed recently?
    - Will you get paid on sales already in the pipeline or only on new deals you bring to the table?
    - Will you get paid on sales from existing customers or only on new customers you bring in?
    - How often is the variable compensation paid?
    - Is it paid when the PO is signed, when the product is shipped, or when the invoice is paid?
    - If the variable pay is a bonus, is there a formula tied to key performance indicators (KPIs) you have to hit, or is it completely arbitrary and dependent entirely on the mood of the hiring manager?
    - Is there a draw involved, and is it just an advance on future commission (called a recoverable draw, because the company recovers its advance payment), or is it non-recoverable (you won't have to pay it back)?
    - Are there any stock options? If yes, is it a one-time award, or can additional equity be earned? How diluted is the equity situation?
- How often are performance evaluations conducted? When will the first one be?
- Does the company provide a cell phone and laptop, or do you use your own? If you use your own, do they give you an allowance to offset your cost?
- What are the employee benefits?
    - What do the health, dental, and vision insurance look like?
    - How much do they cost and when do they start?
    - What does the network of doctors look like? Is your doctor in the network?
    - Do they have flexible spending accounts for childcare and out-of-pocket healthcare expenses?
- Is there paid time off? Are vacation time and sick leave combined into a single allowance, or are they separate?
- Is there short- and long-term disability?
- Is there a 401(k) plan, and when can you start contributing to it?
    - Does the company contribute to the plan?
    - How long do you have to be employed before they start contributing?
- Is there a tuition reimbursement program? What are the terms of reimbursement and forgiveness?
- Is there a company car?
    - Is there a selection of models from which to choose, or do you get what you're given?
    - When would you likely receive the car? If there's a delay, will they provide a temporary vehicle?
- How are business expenses reimbursed?
    - Do you have a company credit card, or do you cover the expenses, then submit for reimbursement?
    - Once you've submitted an expense report, how fast do you get reimbursed?

The Offer

How to Avoid Leaving Money on the Table

An offer can be verbal or written, and you have three options: you can accept, decline, or counter. If you feel the offer is as much as you're likely to get and you do want the job, then go ahead and accept. If you feel there might be more dollars or benefits to gain, then you can counter, but you must do so carefully.

First of all, say thank you for the offer.

> Thank you so much for the offer. I'm very interested in joining the team, and feel it's a super opportunity. I have just a few questions.

Then you should list *all* your questions at the same time. Don't keep going back to the well. Here are some examples of how to phrase questions.

- Is there any paid vacation time?
- Could the vacation be three weeks instead of two? I currently have three weeks and would like to stay at this level.
- How does the company handle sick leave?
- May I have a copy of the benefits summary plus the insurance costs?
- When can I start contributing to the 401(k)?
- Instead of a base salary of $85K, could the base be $90K?
- The base is listed as $100K with a guaranteed annual bonus of $20K. Would it be possible for the base to be $110K and the guaranteed bonus be $10K?
- The hourly rate is listed as $15, and I was wondering if it could be $18 per hour?
- The title is listed as Manager, but in order to gain appropriate access to the right level of customers, could the title be Director?
- Could there be a relocation allowance to fund my move to the new location?
- I'll be leaving $20K commission on the table and wondered if there could be a signing bonus to help bridge the gap.

Returning to a Former Employer

If you're going back to work at a place you've already worked, then ask if your previous tenure can be added to your new employment. It might mean additional vacation or faster vesting.

Working as a Consultant

If a company wants to hire you as a consultant before becoming a full-time employee, try to negotiate the follow-on full-time salary at the same time you negotiate the consulting rate. You have the most leverage and negotiating power prior to starting work, so try to settle the dollar details beforehand.

> Don't be wishy-washy, and don't drag things out. Just make your decision, and don't look back. If you have to cut your hand off, it's better to do it quickly with a sharp knife than to saw at it with a cafeteria spork.

Stories from the Trenches…

One manager said he wished he could ride shotgun with sales candidates because he felt the best sales reps were aggressive drivers who cut people off, weren't always polite, and gunned the engine at a yellow light. Candidates who were more polite on the road would likely be good account managers.

The Offer

Pay Frequency
It's important to find out how often you'll get paid and when you'll see that first paycheck. If you're used to biweekly paychecks but your new employer pays monthly, you'll need to factor that into your budget so you don't get caught short.

Get It in Writing!
No matter how much you like and trust the hiring manager, you should GET THE OFFER IN WRITING! This is not negotiable. If you go on a handshake agreement, you will lose out.

A good way to create an audit trail is to email the hiring manager and detail your understanding of the offer. CC yourself so a copy bounces to your email, then keep that email in the do-not-delete file.

If a company won't commit your offer to writing, then whatever you've been promised is just smoke and mirrors, and you should run, not walk, to the nearest exit.

Once You're Ready to Accept
Thank the hiring manager or recruiter for the offer; say you're very happy to accept and are looking forward to joining the company and being part of the team.
- Ask what the next steps are for the background check, drug screen, and onboarding.
- Ask if you'll receive a formal all-clear-to-start from Human Resources, and if you should wait to resign from your current role until that all-clear is received.
- Ask what start date they want. It's totally okay for you to ask for a different date; just explain why you're asking.

A Leopard Will Never Change Its Spots
Beware the company that extends you a cheap offer. They will always be cheap, and they will never truly value you or your contribution.

How to Decline
If you're not going to take the offer, don't drag things out. Just be gracious, thank the interviewer for the offer, and explain why you can't accept. The hiring company might inquire as to why, and if there is a chance your mind could be changed, have an honest discussion. If your mind is made up, though, just put a full stop on the conversation, and let them move on.

> If the reason to take another job is only about money, and absolutely nothing else, you need to stay put and just ask for a raise.

Stories from the Trenches...

A sales and business development candidate was earning a base salary of $93K and total earnings of $120K to $130K, depending on the year. He said he'd accept a base of $110K and the chance to earn another $20K in commission, and that exact offer was extended, but he countered with a dissertation-length email and the demand for a base of $140K to $160K, a signing bonus between $15K to $20K, a guaranteed bonus for his first year, the same vacation as the executive team, and a severance package equivalent to the combined base and bonus.

The only question remaining in my mind was whether or not he wanted a pony too.

Resigning

Leave Well

If you're currently employed, then you need to give your employer at least two weeks' notice. If you extend your resignation and your boss shows you the door, then you can go back to your new employer and see if they'll let you start earlier. Do not burn bridges, no matter how much you'd like to, because your current employer becomes a reference as soon as you leave.

Sample Resignation Letter

As with the cover letters and thank-you notes, there are a ton of samples online. Whatever you write, just be professional and courteous. No swear words, no insults, no threats. Just be mature and move on.

Here's one sample.

> Dear _____
> After careful consideration, I've decided to accept an opportunity with another company, and my last day with _____ will be two weeks from now on the _____.
>
> I really appreciate the opportunity to have worked at ___ and have learned a great deal here. I wish you all the best.
>
> Sincerely,

Even if You Hate the Place...Keep Your Mouth Shut

Refrain from providing unsolicited feedback during your resignation period. If your current employer wants your opinion, they'll ask. It's just best to quietly move on to your next job, and let your future success be sweet revenge.

The Counteroffer

If you do decide to accept a counteroffer and stay with your current company, the reasons that motivated you to interview elsewhere in the first place haven't changed. You will always be the employee who wanted to leave, so your loyalty is now in question and you might even find yourself at the top of the downsizing list during the next round of budget cuts.

Lisa Quast wrote a super article for Forbes magazine (July 7, 2014) in which she lays out all the reasons you should never take the counter. Just Google "Lisa Quast" and "Why You Should Never Accept A Counter Offer." It's an excellent read.

Do still continue to be present and productive during your resignation; you were hired to do a job, and to not do that is to steal your employer's time and your own self-respect.

Do start taking your belongings home, bit by bit, so you won't have to haul a box home on your last day.

> **Stories from the Trenches...**
>
> A comment from a reference: "He's not lazy; he just lacks vision and knowledge about how to navigate out of a situation."

Job-Hopping

The Merry-Go-Round
If you've updated your résumé, taken a good hard look at your career choices, and come to the conclusion that you've been a member of the job-of-the-month club, could it now be time to get off that merry-go-round? To help ensure you don't keep making the same mistake over and over, you have to figure out the reason for the hopping.

Be honest with yourself, and take stock of your skills. What do you like to do? What do you not like to do? What decisions have you made that put you in this job-of-the-month club cycle in the first place? Have you just made poor choices, or is there something else that has caused these short job stints?

Ask yourself a few questions.

- Have your reasons for leaving only been about earning more money?
- Do you feel sidelined or marginalized?
- Did you, at some point, feel part of the group but now feel like an outsider?
- Is there always someone at work who grates on your nerves?
- Have you noticed a change in how people react to you?
- Have you left multiple jobs because your boss didn't understand you?

I am in no way a psychologist. I have zero training and zero credibility in the field, so these questions are just a way for you to start evaluating your situation. Find someone to talk to: a family member, friend, colleague, former boss, neighbor, minister, help line. If the first person you talk to doesn't help, don't give up. Even if it takes a dozen conversations, keep seeking answers.

Reentry into the Workforce following Sporadic Employment
If your employment has been sporadic but now you want to carve out a more deliberate path, temporary job services can be a super option. If you sign up with a temp service and you go on, say, three week-long assignments over a two-month period, that temporary service is the employer for all three assignments, and you can list continuous employment on your résumé.

You can sign up for multiple temp services at the same time, and this can be a great way to test run a variety of companies and jobs while gaining overall experience.

It Might Not Take Massive Change
People tend to gravitate towards what they like to do, so you might already be close to the right role and don't need to totally reinvent yourself. Maybe it'll just take a few minor tweaks.

The Least Expensive Thing to Change
The fastest way to change your situation is to change how you're viewing things. It's free and instantaneous!

The best way to change your outlook is to practice being other-focused instead of self-focused. It's tough to think about your own interests and those of someone else at the same time, so being other-focused can help reduce your own angst.

Just start simple, and work on your communication skills one conversation at a time. You'll feel better at the end of the day, be much more in control of your situation, and be more likely to see opportunities you might previously have overlooked,

> **Stories from the Trenches...**
>
> Reply from a manager when I asked how the new hire was settling in: "We've cut the top off the fire hydrant and shoved his face in it."

You're a Young Adult Just Starting Out

But I'm Just a Kid!

As a senior in high school, you're asked, "Where are you going to college?" and "What do you want to be?" You smile politely and mumble something, but in your head you're screaming, "How should I know?" Right now, you don't have enough experience to even begin to gauge your options, but you might have an inkling of what you would hate to do all day long. So really, a better question to ask you would be, "What do you *not* want to be?"

Don't worry so much about the college you select. Yes, your parents, guidance counselors, teachers, and "people who know best" will tell you it's *all* about the college you attend. But it really isn't. It's actually all about hard work, industriousness, good manners, and intent. First, you need to learn how to *make* decisions, and then you have to learn how to make *good* decisions on a consistent basis, and no institution of higher learning will have these things in its curriculum. It's just stuff you have to learn on your own.

You could skip college altogether or go to a tiny community college out in the middle of nowhere, and still go on to be a raving success and a mover and shaker in the world. Alternatively, you could go to a top-ranked school but end up failing dismally.

Case in point: One of the most compelling education paths I've ever seen on a résumé was of an early-career product manager. He came from a single-parent home, and there was no money for college, so he self-funded his education by working full time during the day and attending college at night. It took him four years to complete a two-year associate's degree. It took him another four years to complete the bachelor's degree. It then took him four more years to complete a two-year MBA program. In all, it took him twelve years to complete what most would have done in six. But he came out of school with zero debt and a track record of perseverance that is exceedingly rare.

The bottom line is, it's not the school you attend that makes the difference. It's just you and how hard you work, your character, your integrity, your intent, and your honor. Whatever you choose to do, just work harder than anyone else, and the money *will* follow.

Your First Job

Your first job out of school doesn't define you. It truly is just a single step in a very long journey.

If you've just entered the workforce and the only job available is, say, driving a forklift in a warehouse, then take it. It'll be money in the bank, you'll learn a cool skill, and it'll highlight your work ethic and willingness to take on any job necessary. Who cares if your old high school buddies think it's a schlump job? You'll be employed with money coming in the door. Plus, you just never know what kind of springboard that job will become.

My Pitch for Community College

Not everyone needs a bachelor's degree. In fact, the way the world is right now, you might just have greater earnings potential if you go into a trade as opposed to a professional job.

The Best Advice I Can Give You

Work really hard, become an expert in those mundane tasks no one else wants to do, be willing to go the extra mile, be nice to everyone, and be thankful for what you have instead of complaining about what you lack. Whatever the task, aim for excellence. If you're cleaning the toilet…make it gleam. Hard work and an honorable attitude always pay off in the end.

It's okay to make a lot of mistakes…just don't keep making the same ones over and over.

A Note from Jane

Dear Reader,

My deepest wish is that I've been of some help to you in your job search. I hope you've found some golden nuggets of information, had a few aha! moments, and even laughed out loud a couple of times. All those "Stories from the Trenches" are true…you just can't make this stuff up.

On your darkest days, just breathe and keep putting one foot in front of the other. Patience and perseverance are better than gold, and they will carry you forward. Never, ever give up. Just keep going, and you will step out into the sunshine and into a great new job when you least expect it.

Thank you for your time and for letting me walk this journey with you, and I wish you the absolute best of success in all your future endeavors.

Cheers,

Jane

Job Search Daily Activity Log

Job Search	Monday	Tuesday	Wednesday	Thursday	Friday
Start time					
Lunch					
End time					
Total time searching					
Resume submissions (5 points each)					
Follow-up on existing submissions (1 point each)					
Talk to anyone about the search (5 points each)					
Phone interview (10 points each)					
In-person interview (20 points each)					
Volunteering (10 points each)					
Total points — Goal is 25 points per day					

Daily Goal: Get a job offer **OR** schedule an interview **OR** achieve 25 points

Disclaimer: The author make no guarantees concerning the level of success you may experience by following the advice and strategies contained in this book. Results will differ for each individual. The testimonials and examples provided in this book show individual results, which may not apply to any other individual, and are not intended to represent or guarantee that you will achieve the same or similar results.

Acknowledgements

To Steve, my wonderful husband, for always believing in me.

To my sons, Christopher and David, for their awesome input and support.

To Jerry Byrnes, for reading the very first draft (and numerous drafts thereafter) and whose feedback set the foundation for the rest of the journey.

To Bob Mosler, my fabulous eagle-eyed longtime compadre in recruiting, who cheerfully slogged through several drafts and caught a thousand errors.

To my dear friend Beth McFadyen, for reading the drafts and whose encouragement was better than gold.

To Jacob McFadyen, Christopher Snipes, David Snipes, Charly Brüggenjürgen, Lukas Palaske, and Cheng Ji, for providing the LinkedIn sample pictures.

To Craig Scachitti and Brian Gold, the first to put the résumé instructions to use, for their fantastic feedback.

To Bill Greenleaf of Greenleaf Literary Services, Inc., proofreader extraordinaire and the first literary professional to read the manuscript, whose feedback made my year.

To Layne Walker of New Friends Publishing, LLC, for his awesome help and guidance in getting this endeavor over the finish line.

To Lindsey Carpenter for her InDesign wizardry.

And to all the amazing people I've talked with in the recruiting process, and without whom this book would never have come to be.

Made in the USA
Columbia, SC
20 March 2021